THE
3D TYPE
BOOK

LAURENCE KING

Published in 2011 by
Laurence King Publishing Ltd
361–373 City Road
London EC1V 1LR
United Kingdom
email: enquiries@laurenceking.com
www.laurenceking.com

A catalogue record for this book
is available from the British Library.

ISBN: 978-185669-713-2

Words and image selection:
Agathe Jacquillat and
Tomi Vollauschek at FL@33

Front cover images:
'3' by Atelier van Wageningen
'D' by Dolly Rogers
'T' and
'Y' by HandMadeFont
'P' by Rafael Farias
'E' by Andrew Byrom

Book design: FL@33
www.flat33.com

Printed in China

THE 3D TYPE BOOK

AGATHE JACQUILLAT AND TOMI VOLLAUSCHEK AT FL@33

LAURENCE KING PUBLISHING

CONTENTS

FOREWORD: Type as Object by Andrew Byrom

'3D' – a buzzword of our time – is most often used to describe something that is actually flat but has the *effect*, or gives the illusion, of depth. Developments in 3D technology have revitalized the movie industry in recent years, with feature films such as *Avatar* pointing to a new era of submersive storytelling. Interactive virtual software has irreversibly changed the working methods of surgeons, engineers, architects and automobile designers. And around the corner is the often promised, and perhaps soon to be fully realized, real-time holographic projection.

This trend towards 3D can also be seen in contemporary graphic design. Many designers began to take notice of this graphic phenomenon when UPS unveiled a new logo, designed by FutureBrand, in 2003. The previous logo, designed by Paul Rand in 1961, was a line-art image of a string-bound paper box placed above the letters 'UPS', combining to create a shield. Like other iconic logos from that time, it was an exercise in graphic reduction, forced by the limitations of the production technology of the day.

The proliferation of full-colour printing, and the reality that logos are now presented more and more on screen, means that in recent years these constraints have fallen away. Although the redesigned UPS logo retains the overall shield motif, it is now full-colour, has highlights, shadow and shade, and, most notably, is presented as if it were a physical object.

Countless businesses have followed suit. Look around: AT&T, ABC, Chevron, Ford, Hewlett-Packard, Xerox and many other long-standing corporate icons have been replaced by generic, bulbous reinterpretations.

Typeface design too has been caught up in a 3D trend; however, instead of the slick lens flares, shadows and pseudo-realism of the contemporary logo, type designers seem to be edging away from a digital aesthetic towards a more hands-on approach.

The computer-generated experiments of the early years of digital type design were – for good or bad – fundamentally shaped by both the limitations and possibilities of this new technology. For example, the work of Zuzana Licko at Emigre, or the majority of the designs produced for Neville Brody's FUSE project, seemed to celebrate these new-found digital properties. Other designers, given the tools of typeface design for the first time (through programs like Fontographer), took a more direct approach. The following decade saw many examples of bastardized classic typefaces, either with subtle changes or, more often, the obliteration of an existing design by stretching points or adding visual clutter – perhaps laying the seeds for the period of 'grunge' typography that would follow.

For many years, these reactions became the overriding graphic aesthetic. The effect that the Macintosh had on typography in the 1990s is similar to the impact that synthesized sound had on music in the mid-1970s.

Three Tragedies, 1948
Alvin Lustig
This page, top: Hand lettering was prominent on book covers of the 1940s and 1950s, notably in the work of Paul Rand and Alvin Lustig. The hand-lettered image featured on this iconic Lustig cover design was actually created and shot on Santa Monica beach in California by his wife, Elaine Lustig Cohen. It is a perfect example of how 3D lettering can evoke a personal and emotional response.

Xybion logo, 1975
Louis Danziger
This page, centre: Designed some nine years before Apple introduced the Macintosh, Danziger's mark was the first commercial logo to be designed on a computer. It was plotted and drawn on California Institute of Technology's mainframe computer.

Calypso font, 1958
Roger Excoffon
Left, bottom: A Letraset favourite, *Calypso* became a classic display font of the 1970s. Reminiscent, perhaps, of a contemporary Frank Gehry building, its three-dimensional system seems abstract. As such, it is harder to dissect than, for example, Glaser's design (above).

With the contemporary trend towards physical typography, Roger Excoffon's *Calypso* cries out to be constructed. Fabricated by Clay Cooper, Jack Curry, Shantelle David, Sungoh Lim, Abheeth Salgado and Eugene Takagi (with art direction from Andrew Byrom), these paper models were created to illustrate how the *Calypso* letterforms would work as physical objects.

We're Sorry, 2009
Marian Bantjes
This page, top: *We're Sorry*, an illustration for the cover of *The Walrus* magazine, 2009. Art directors: Kelsey Blackwell/Brian Morgan. Bantjes' pencil crayon drawing of entangled yarn plays in the middle ground between 2D and 3D lettering.

Babycurls, 1970
Milton Glaser
This page, bottom: Milton Glaser's design seems almost like a diagram for 3D construction, with sections cut from a simple tube. Client: Photolettering; lettering execution: George Leavitt.

For several years, this new computer-generated sound permeated popular music. In many cases, it completely replaced traditional instruments. Digital technology no longer tried to reproduce pre-existing sound. It had created its own. This synthetic sound became the overriding trend into the 1980s. But after time the synthesizer found its place as another tool, another instrument among many.

Similarly, decades after its introduction, the computer seems to have found its place in relation to typeface design. Today, the Mac is like the oven to a chef or the kiln to a potter: it is a tool for construction, delivery and output. Designers thrive on limitations and on working around, and through, constraints. As the computer no longer seems to possess these limitations, designers are now looking elsewhere for new forms, new boundaries and new problems to solve.

Typographic design is going through a post-digital reaction. The recent handmade trend, with letterforms being constructed more and more in three dimensions, seems to support this idea.

The work gathered in *The 3D Type Book* plays with an unmapped middle ground. This is not just, for example, 'Helvetica' rendered in pebbles, neckties, venetian blinds, socks or cheese (yes, cheese – turn to page 140), but instead a reaction to the limitations and constraints of unexpected materials and processes that help shape – or often force – the outcome.

There is often a distinction made between lettering and typeface design. A typeface is a comprehensive collection of characters that belong together; a system. When used to set words on a page, type, by its very nature, is unchanged by the message it purveys. The letters of a typeface are designed to relate to each other, not to the unknown words they will ultimately communicate.

Lettering, on the other hand, is often more idiosyncratic, expressive, spontaneous and free to be affected by its message.

Perhaps the work in this publication can also be viewed in similar categories.

3D typography: Designs that manage to cling to typographic conventions, such as a universal x-height, baseline, proportions and so on. Examples of this are the typography created for the artist Skin by Shotopop (page 201) and the *Typelace* typeface, constructed by Rafael Farias using the (dot matrix-like) grid found in the laces and grommets on a pair of shoes (page 184).

3D lettering: Here objects are found, arranged and/or manipulated to create letters. Examples of this include Clotilde Olyff's *Pebbles*, a series of found objects collected over 20 years (pages 58–59, 60), and Jörger-Stauss's *Days of Literature* (page 116), where yarn replaces the line

of a pen. The work of Stefan Sagmeister looms large in this area. From his lettering constructed out of clothes and fabric for a 1999 catalogue for fashion designer Anni Kuan, to the title sequence for *The Happy Film* (page 200), Sagmeister has had a profound effect on our current hand-built aesthetic.

Another fascinating trend that appears throughout this book (and in both areas mentioned above) is that of typographic 'performance'.

This work exudes a sense of time, movement or narrative. An example of this is Hijack Your Life's *Backbreaker* (page 96), which shows performers acting out letters in the wind using their bodies and billowing fabric. In Amandine Alessandra's *Letterform for the Ephemeral* (pages 14–15), type is 'wearable' and words are shown *performed* in public spaces.

Like many other examples in this book, MoreGood's beautiful *Waterform* design (pages 160–161) allows the viewer in on its process. And although the moment of capturing the image is vital, we are left to imagine what follows the second after the camera's shutter opens.

Some images are literally stills from live-action films. Some examples include Pleaseletmedesign's *iQ* font, constructed by marks made by the wheels of a car (pages 176–177); Sean Martindale's *Nature* (page 192), and Miguel Ramirez's *Morph* (page 140), where we see hands grating cheese as a word appears on another dot matrix-like grid, that of a cheese grater.

Traditionally, typography is bound by the page. When type is taken away from its printed form and presented as a three-dimensional object, many historic conventions seem no longer to apply. Perhaps the term '3D' is out of place in this book. This is not the *effect* of three dimensions; these are actual objects. In relation to a 3D movie, the work that FL@33 has compiled here is theatre. There is no illusion. There is no need for blue and red glasses. This is type as object; physical and *real*.

Creation, 2009
April Larivee
This page, top, left: A striking example of three-dimensional lettering that rejects traditional typographic convention (unified stroke width, form, x-height and so on) and lets the chosen material dictate everything.

Vogue magazine cover, August 1940
Horst
This page, top, right: An iconic example of performance typography that has been echoed in recent years. Picture: Horst/Vogue © The Condé Nast Publications Ltd.

Commune (Alphabet), 1991–ongoing
Paul Elliman
This page, bottom, left and centre: Here Elliman is in the role of director, casting the part and coaxing a performance. Although originally conceived as part of Neville Brody's FUSE project, Elliman's *Commune* design was always an oddity, and never seemed to belong to that period.

Where most experimental type designs of the early to mid-1990s tended to be reactions to the newly acquired, and ultimately ephemeral, aesthetic of early digital technology, Elliman's collection of letters/images has a timeless quality, where concept trumps style.

Haiti Relief poster, 2010
Kari Szentesi
This page, bottom, right: Designed as part of a student project (CSULB) to raise awareness of the relief effort underway after the 2010 earthquake in Haiti, Szentesi's design illustrates the immediacy and impact of handmade lettering. Here, type and image become unified; the word adds meaning to the three-dimensional objects, while the objects suggest a haunting narrative to the word. It is hard to imagine the word 'Haiti' set in any other typeface, or lettering style, having the same effect.

INTRODUCTION

Thanks to Andrew Byrom's insightful foreword, we can focus in this introduction on FL@33's own influences, why we created this book and how.

Many of FL@33's own typographic experiments over the years have involved real 3D lettering and illustrated 3D type. Come to think of it, this is something we have been fascinated with since childhood, enjoying plenty of alphabet soup and, in the late 1970s and early 1980s, the daily dose of the colourful, often talking, letters that walked and danced through the scenes of children's television programme *Sesame Street*. Surely everybody would fall in love with three-dimensional typography if they saw a letter 'M' with eyes start munching away at everything on the screen – saying *'Mmmmm'* in the process – or Cookie Monster eating all the 3D letters Ernie introduced to his audience. If you add to the mix of influences things like the iconic Hollywood sign in Los Angeles that everybody knows, or the public signage we are all surrounded with, it becomes clear that 3D type is something we are all exposed to. Combined with a new wave of appreciation for everything non-digital, handmade and well-crafted, designers and artists have created a massive body of work involving three-dimensional typography over the last few decades.

Therefore, it did not come as a big surprise that so many fellow designers and artists share our fascination with 3D type, and we received such positive feedback when we started sourcing the images for this book.

After almost two years in the making, we are now happy to present *The 3D Type Book* – a handbook, source of inspiration and the most comprehensive showcase so far that focuses 100 per cent on three-dimensional experimental letterforms, sculptural shape-shifting letters, tactile experiences and surprising and inventive ways to interpret the alphabet, ranging from beautiful and humorous to poetic, witty and conceptual. In 240 pages, *The 3D Type Book* features over 1,300 pictures illustrating more than 300 projects by more than 160 selected contributors from around the world.

Like no other previous publication, *The 3D Type Book* also features pioneering work from the last century, going back as far as the 1940s. The overall focus, however, is on recent and brand-new typographic projects and experiments – imaginative, playful work with sculptural and three-dimensional letterforms. The book showcases some classic must-haves next to lesser-known yet exciting work, along with some previously unpublished pieces – some even created especially for this book. Self-initiated experiments were as welcome as commissioned projects.

Selected projects include letter-shaped silhouettes of found objects, grid-based multiples, handmade three-dimensional letters, installations and performances, sculptural letterforms, optical illusions and vantage-point experiments, and light and shadow creations, beside many others. A handful of concepts were also included of letterforms that could theoretically have been made and arranged and then photographed, but were only drawn to document the idea. These are a few exceptions, however; almost everything else is tangible.

As with FL@33's previous books, *Postcard* (2008) and *Made & Sold* (2009), we hand-picked many designers and artists who received personal invitations for potential inclusion. In addition, in summer 2009 we launched an open call for entries that was widely published across the internet and sent to thousands of our newsletter subscribers, Twitter and Facebook followers. We had an overwhelming response; over 500 3D type projects from more than 250 individuals and studios were submitted – over 100 gigabytes of raw data – and the selection process was particularly challenging given the extraordinarily high quality of the submissions.

The book is divided into letter groups from A to Z. Showcased projects within these sections, however, are not in strict alphabetical order; this allowed us more flexibility in the design of the book.

Like all books that FL@33 has conceived, written, compiled and designed, *The 3D Type Book* also has a dedicated chapter at the end of the book presenting profiles with links to websites of all the individuals and studios behind the showcased creations.

We hope you find this exciting selection of works by these passionate individuals, collectives and studios as inspiring as we do.

Agathe Jacquillat and Tomi Vollauschek, FL@33, 2011.

THE QUICK BROWN FOX JUMPS OVER A LAZY DOG

Feature
Antoine+Manuel
Left: Paris-based Antoine Audiau and Manuel Warosz produced this typeface box set from 2008 in a limited edition of five. It is entitled *Feature*, made of laser-cut Perspex 60 x 50cm (24 x 20in), and was produced for Antoine+Manuel's exhibition at the Musée des Arts Décoratifs, Paris, which ran from January to May 2009.

Book as Block
Amandine Alessandra
Above: Amandine Alessandra is a French photographer and graphic designer based in London. This project was inspired by Thomas Fuller's statement, *'A book that is shut is but a block'* The shelves were used as a typographic grid, while the books were selected for their shape and colour rather than their content. Building up the letters reminded Amandine of typesetting; every letter made of coloured books had to be blocked with white

books, just as in letterpress, where large areas of white space are created by wooden blocks called 'furniture'.

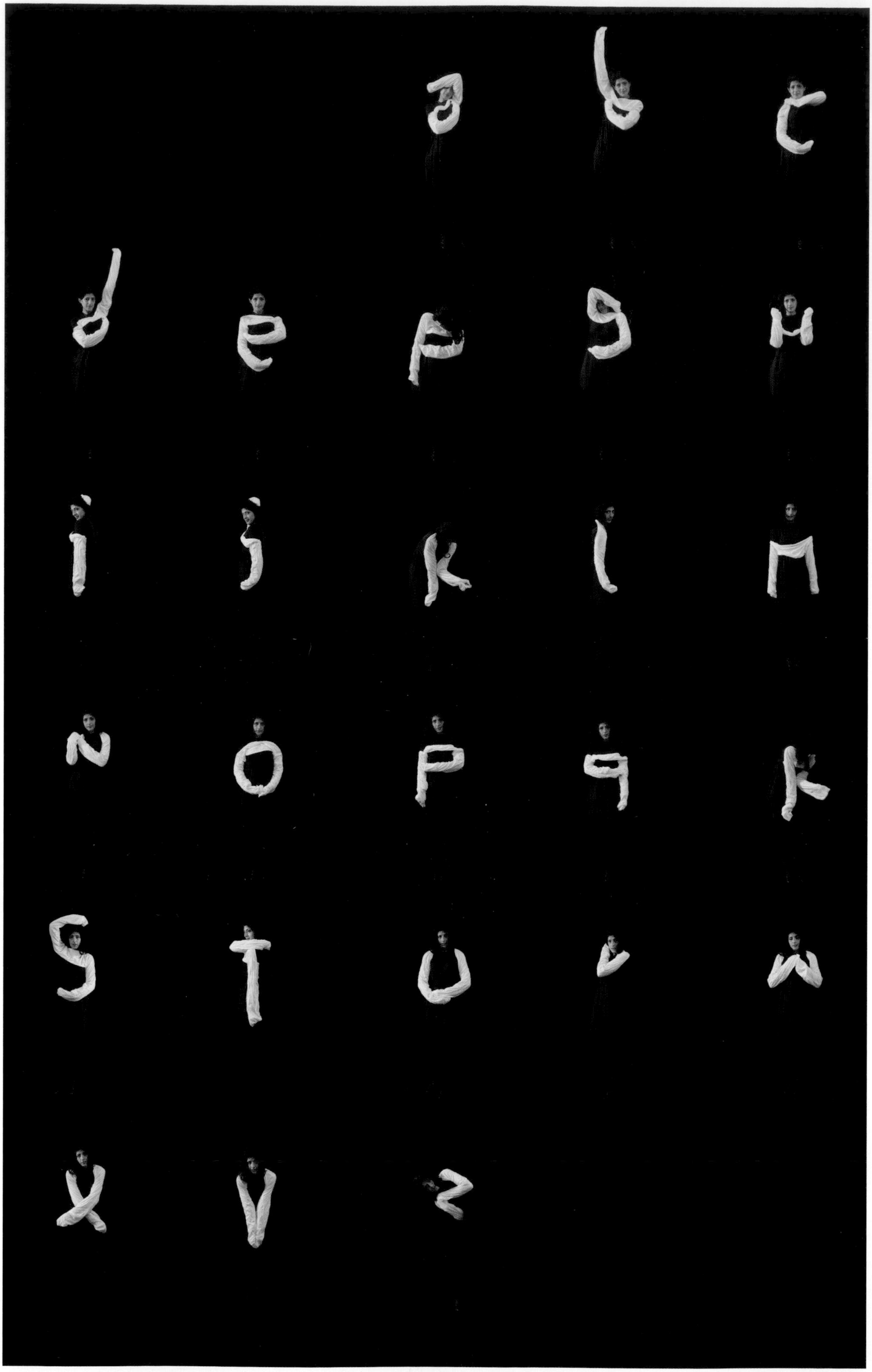

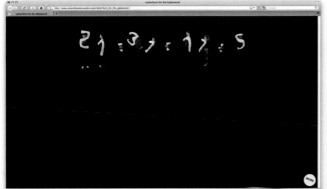

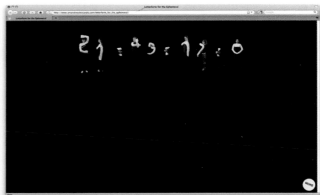

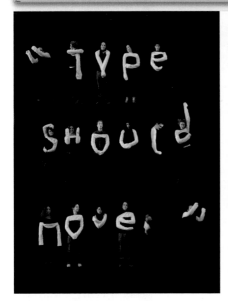

Letterform for the Ephemeral
Amandine Alessandra

Amandine Alessandra's project *Letterform for the Ephemeral* consists of several phases, all of which were created between 2009 and 2010. The experiment started with wearable typography. Amandine created so-called *boleros* – a pair of day-glo sleeves – and then attached them together with a strip of fabric so that they could be worn across the front or the back of the wearer. These sleeves allowed the wearer to form any letter or number in a small move. Once all the wearable letters were ready, Amandine used the ephemeral typography to induce people to feel the weight of passing time, with its flow symbolically interrupted by halting the traffic. This typographic performance was recorded by taking screenshots of the images transmitted by a public webcam showing the iconic Abbey Road crossing in London – site of the famous Beatles' album cover (http://abbeyroad.com/visit). The next phase was a clock – a choreographed performance referencing the (real) passing of time. The people standing as the hours moved only once every 60 minutes, while the one acting as the tenths of seconds executed a very fast routine in a continual move. Following the clock idea, a performance then took place in a busy train station during rush hour. It involved eight people mimicking a digital clock in real time using the movements of their arms and shoulders.

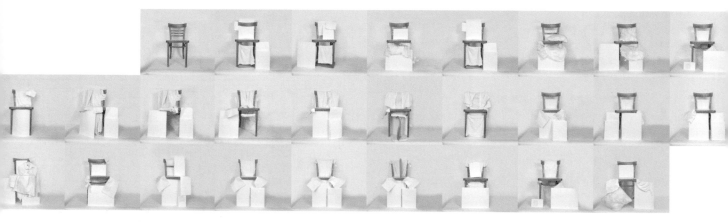

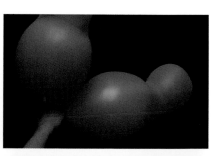

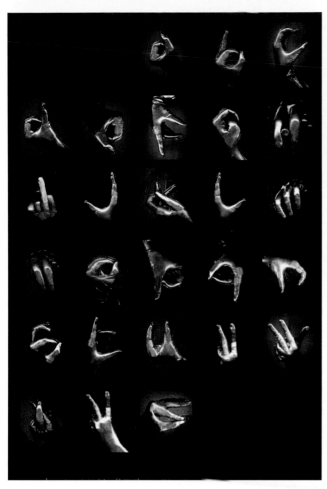

Ephemeral stencils
Amandine Alessandra
Left, top: In 2009, Amandine used a stencil to set the word 'ALWAYS' in 1296 point, first using salt, then breadcrumbs on grass.

Take a Seat
Amandine Alessandra
Left, centre: *Take a Seat*, from 2009, uses a chair as a matrix for an alphabet. Each letter is a meaningless installation if seen on its own, but becomes decipherable when a few are put

together to form words. Objects become readable.

Wow/Light
Amandine Alessandra
Left, bottom: These were experiments from 2009 for temporary high-visibility typographic installations.

Maîtresse alphabet
Amandine Alessandra
This page, top, left: This alphabet from 2009 was made by photographing hands encased in shiny PVC gloves.

Body type
Amandine Alessandra
This page, top, right: The *Body type* alphabet from 2009 was an experiment into organic letterforms emerging when reframing the body. It uses the analogy between typesetting terminology and vocabulary for the human body, for example: anatomy, body size, head piece, footers, leg, eye, arms, chin and hairline.

I Have Proved
Amandine Alessandra
This page, bottom: The original quote, *'I have proved by actual trial that a letter, that takes an hour to write, takes only about 3 minutes to read!'*, by Lewis Carroll, was written in the context of the lost art of handwritten correspondence. This installation was from 2009.

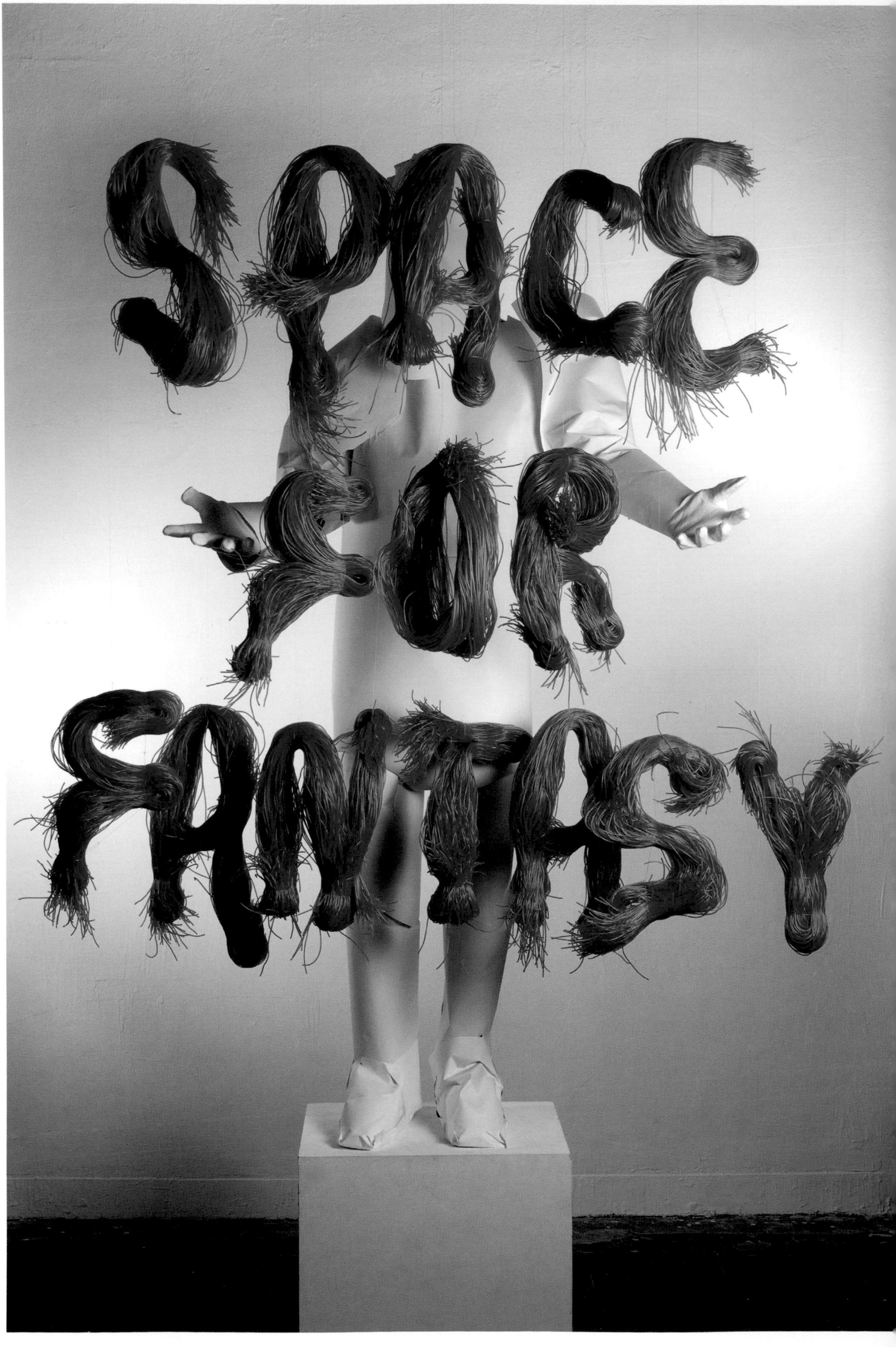
SPACE
FOR
FANTASY

Space for Fantasy
Akatre
Left: French design studio Akatre was founded by Valentin Abad, Julien Dhivert and Sebastien Riveron. This visual was created for Space for Fantasy – an art exhibition held at Paris' Galerie des Galeries (Galeries Lafayette) in 2010.

A4
Akatre
This page, top: The three Akatre members perform a letter A/ number 4 hybrid to illustrate their name, Akatre, which means A4 (*à quatre*) when pronounced in French. Asked – why four? – when there are only three of them, they reply that the fourth member is considered to be the client and/or collaborator.

Mains d'Œuvres
Akatre
This page, bottom: These typographic pieces were created for Akatre's client Mains d'Œuvres (a venue and cultural centre). They were used as motifs on flyers for part of the company's 2007/08 print campaign. The visuals were created with sugar cubes.

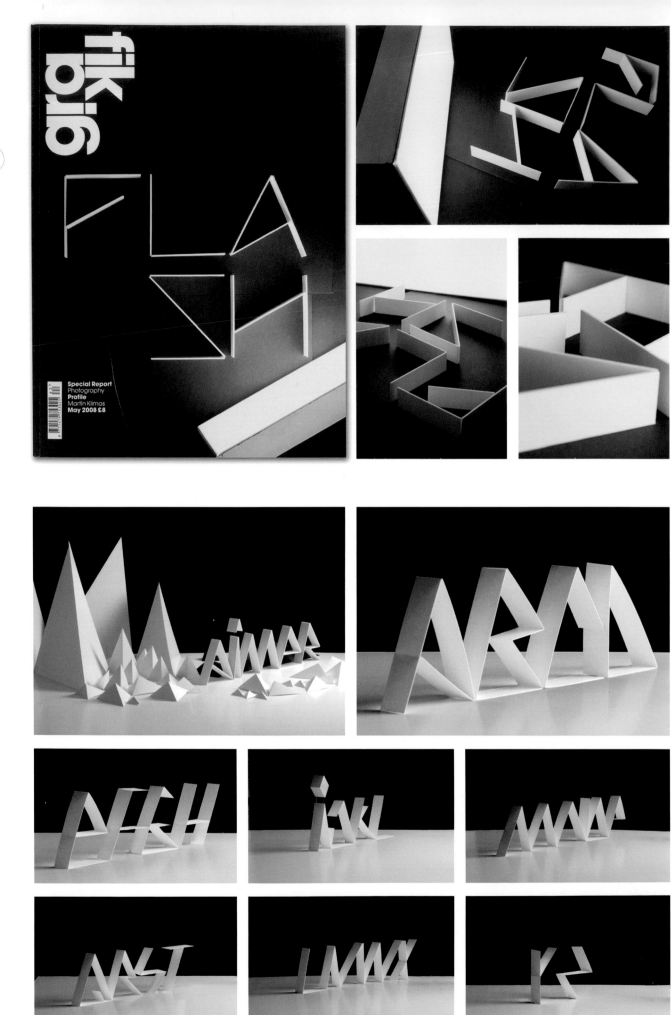

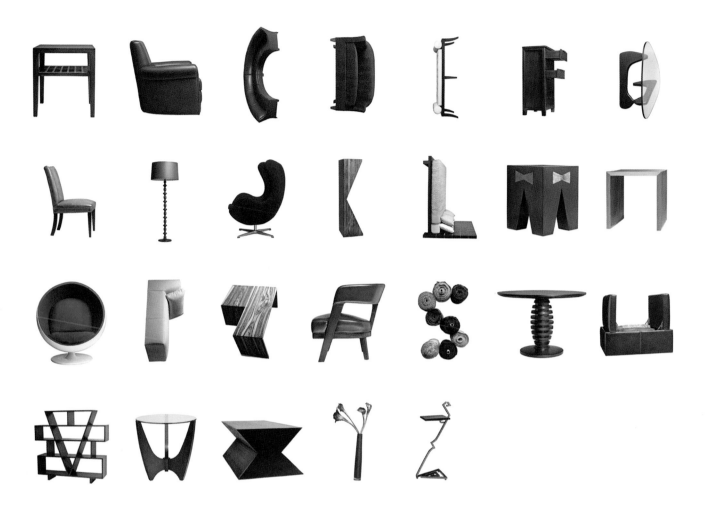

Grafik cover

Akatre

Left, top: Akatre designed this front cover for London-based *Grafik* magazine, number 162, May 2008, that featured a special report on photography.

Mains d'Œuvres

Akatre

Left, bottom: Experimental lettering commissioned by Mains d'Œuvres. The visual featuring the spikey pyramids was used for a programme that also formed part of the 2007/08 campaign – like the sugar cubes pieces shown on the previous page.

Furniture alphabet

Adam Voorhes

This page, top: Photographer Adam Voorhes is based in Austin, Texas. His furniture alphabet for furniture store High Fashion Home in Houston, Texas, was originally published in print and outdoor ads in February 2008. The project was a collaboration with creative communications firm The Butler Bros. Concepting: Stephanie Chan; art directors: Cody Haltom, Adam Mendez.

Austin Monthly magazine cover

Adam Voorhes

This page, bottom: The 'Help Wanted' copy was published as the cover of *Austin Monthly* magazine, which also featured the artwork as the opener of their June 2009 issue. Art director and stylist: Robin Finlay.

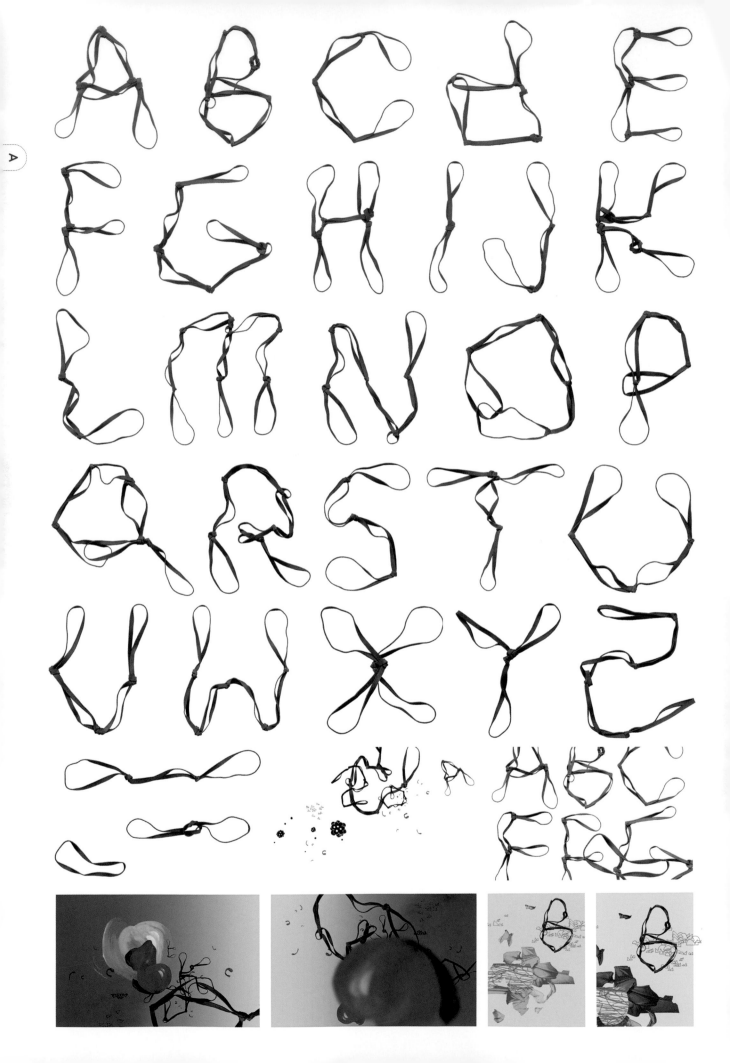

Rubber band typeface
Alexander Egger

Left: This is a previously unpublished colour version of the *Rubber Band* typeface by Italian-born, Vienna-based graphic designer Alexander Egger. Below are a few of the visual experiments that Alexander is best known for.

Trash type
Anna Garforth and Eleanor Stevens

This page, top: Freelance designer, illustrator and environmental artist Anna Garforth runs creative practice Abe in London. Her *Trash* type was the product of a collaborative workshop taught by Anna and Eleanor Stevens at London College of Communication. They worked with second-year graphic design students to create a word communicating the medium. The medium was trash, and the word they chose was 'used'. A week's worth of rubbish was collected by the students and turned into the typographic piece.

Rethink
Anna Garforth

This page, bottom: This piece was located in front of two resources that everybody is heavily reliant upon: gas and water. The word communicates a need to rethink what we consume and how we consume it. Additional leaf typography was installed on railings around the city, using only leaves and thorns. An interview about the project was broadcast in 2010 by Arte TV's *Tracks*.

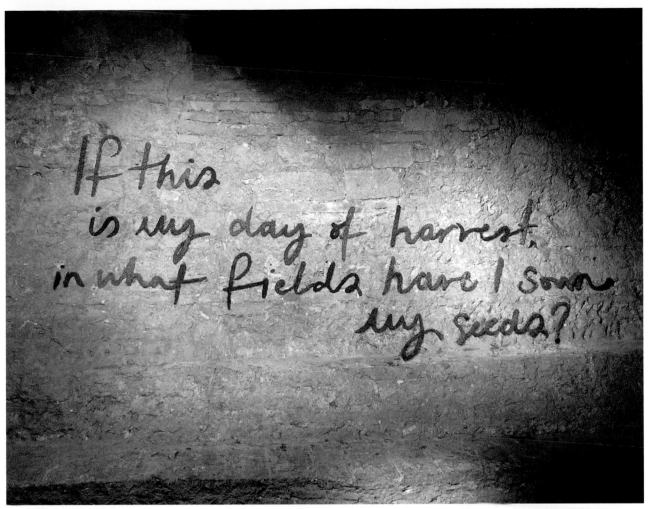

Nourish
**Anna Garforth and
Eleanor Stevens**
Left: This self-initiated collaborative piece was created by Anna Garforth and Eleanor Stevens. The word is 'nourish', and the typeface was handwritten by Eleanor, which the duo then rendered in moss. (*Nourish*: To provide with the substances necessary for growth, health and good condition. From the Latin *nutrire*, 'feed, cherish'. To provide for, sustain, encourage, nurture, cultivate, strengthen, enrich.)

Prophet
**Anna Garforth and
Eleanor Stevens**
This page, top: *Prophet* was another collaboration between Anna and Eleanor Stevens. In spring 2009, the team exhibited in Italy at The Rocca Paolina for the 'Over Design Over' exhibition. They were showcased with 44 other internationally acclaimed artists, including graphic designer Stefan Sagmeister (also featured in this book) and Italian designer Enzo Mari. For this exhibition, the duo illustrated a quote from Kahlil Gibran's *The Prophet*: 'If this is my day of harvest, in what fields have I sown my seeds?'

This page, bottom: A detail of *Prophet* and snapshots of Anna's practice Abe in mossy action.

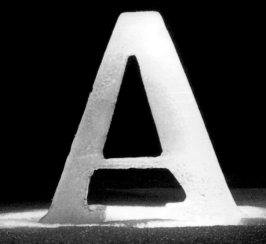

ABOC°
Allistair Burt
Left: Allistair Burt is a multi-disciplinary artist with a background in architecture. He runs Glasgow-based studio Hole in my Pocket. Allistair's work encompasses a wide range of artistic forms such as film, site-specific art, painting, illustration and sculpture. *ABOC°* was created especially for this book, interpreting the alphabet using a temporary and fleeting material: snow.

Fragile
Alex Robbins
This page, top: Berlin-based illustrator and designer Alex Robbins created *Fragile* using a hole punch. It is one of a series of typographic pieces produced for an ongoing self-initiated project in which Alex creates typographic responses to words and phrases. These are selected from various sources, including overheard conversations, magazine articles and Twitter updates.

Urban Intervention – Ice Hands
AT.AW.
This page, bottom: Under the label AT.AW., Toronto-based architect Eric Cheung creates side projects in which he optimistically subverts the often neglected urban environment. In *Ice Hands* (2009) Eric comments on how, in very cold weather, typical of Canadian winters, the act of communication is often 'muffled'. He playfully indicates how people might use sign language to communicate during the winter.

Eureka Tower car park, Melbourne
Axel Peemoeller
Left: Axel Peemoeller developed a wayfinding system for the Eureka Tower car park in Melbourne while working for Emery Studio. The apparently distorted letters on the wall can be read perfectly when standing in the right position. This widely published project from 2006 won several international design awards.

Feld magazine
Axel Peemoeller
This page: Created for *Feld* magazine, these visuals feature poetry by autistic author Birger Sellin.

Top: *'Scurry Birger'*.

Bottom, left: *'I don't really fit into this crazy, cowardly, awful society. It is so weird, this selection of iron aces.'* Followed by two grammatically wrong and more fragmented poems – freely translated – including original

typos: *'Totally without me a fiasco a chaos shiveringly this vast extent resembles a partially dead city of ruins. I participate as destroyer and a disgusting "nonsense-magager".'*

Bottom, right: *'The one and only iron lonely one strives for a first and only iron valuable thought inventing poem'.*

A

ECHTE KERLE

„DER TOD STEHT IHNEN GUT."

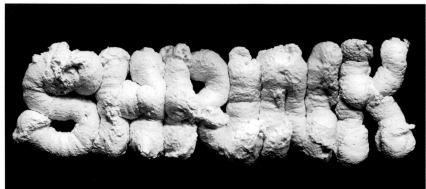

MAGAZINE FOR FASHION AND ART.

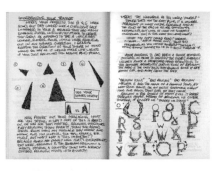

Feld magazine

Axel Peemoeller

Left, top and centre, right: Illustrations for *Feld* magazine's literature section: 'Dead', 'Real Blokes' and 'Death Suits You Well'.

Various magazine contributions

Axel Peemoeller

Left, centre, left and bottom centre: Various magazine contributions featuring three-dimensional type experiments, including the typographic illustration *Dead Man* in the far left, bottom corner, which Axel created for the 'Pirate' issue of a Mexican magazine.

Verve

Axel Peemoeller

Left, bottom, right: Front cover of a printed, large-scale magazine that Axel designed for Verve online and Verve webshop.

Splinter

Arslan Shahid

Above: Toronto-based Arslan Shahid is a graphic design student from OCAD (Ontario College of Art & Design). He created his *Splinter* typeface in 2010 to reflect the concept of war. As a starting point, Arslan took some wise words from his father to heart: *'It takes at least two for war. Conflict, on the other hand, could be within a faction or even within oneself. The outcome of war is destruction, disruption and pain. One cannot reflect war in a symmetric, disciplined and orderly type.'*

A B C D E F G H
I J K L M N O P
Q R S T U V W X
Y Z 0 1 2 3 4 5 6
7 8 9 ! ? . , / @

LIEFDE
GOED GELUK FIJN WIJSHEID SCHAP VRIEND VOL VOOR SPOED SUCCES VREUGDE WELZIJN FIJN GEZOND VREDE VRIJ RIJK GELUK
FORTUIN
VRIEND SCHAP
LIEFDE SUCCES
KUSSEN

VREDE SUCCES KUSSEN WIJSHEID BLIJ VOOR SPOED ROEM VREDE
SUCCES FORTUIN ROEM NON STER FELIJK VRIEND SCHAP GEZOND FORTUIN WIJSHEID SUCCES ROEM GELUK
BLIJ SUCCES FORTUIN GEZOND LIEFDE GELUK
LIEFDE RIJK WIJSHEID FORTUIN LIEFDE GOED KUSSEN GEZOND SPOED VOOR LIEFDE VRIJ VREDE

FC Autobahn regular

ABCDEFGHIJKL
MNOPQRSTUV
WXYZ

abcdefghijklm
nopqrstuvwxyz
1234567890

Pure type

Atelier van Wageningen

Left: Atelier van Wageningen (AVW) is a (typo)graphic design studio based in Amsterdam that has been run by Mark van Wageningen since 1995. Mark regularly publishes (mostly two-dimensional) typefaces, and his fonts are widely available. The idea that *Pure* type could theoretically wither with time intrigues Mark, as a fourth dimension would then be added to this three-dimensional type experiment.

FC Autobahn

Autobahn

Above: In 2008, Jeroen Breen, Rob Stolte and Maarten Dullemeijer from design studio Autobahn in Utrecht, the Netherlands, were invited to design a poster for the Graphic Design Festival Breda (GDFB). During the daytime, the posters demonstrated the concept of graphic design in all its facets, while at night the GDFB logo, printed at the back, shone through the posters. Following a very free brief, Autobahn took the opportunity to demonstrate how work time and spare time can blend very well. During afternoon breaks, Autobahn members often play a game of football in the parking lot next to their studio complex. In wintertime, the table football table in the canteen becomes a meeting point for daily relaxation. Autobahn decided to combine its love for typography and its love of football in this award-winning typographic project, *FC Autobahn*: a font that is based on the markings on a football pitch. The type specimen, which consists of the pangram 'the quick brown fox jumps over the lazy dog', was written on the grass of a football field using a chalk cart. Photos: Jaap Scheeren.

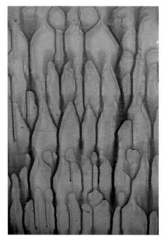

Fig. 3:

Autobahn Geſvetica

Uppercase:
ABCDEFGHIJKLMN
OPQRSTUVWXYZ

Lowercase:
abcdefghijklmnopq
rstuvwxyz

Numbers:
0123456789

NEW

Fig. 1:

Autobahn Heldentica

Uppercase:
ABCDEFGHIJKLM
NOPQRSTUVWXYZ

Lowercase:
abcdefghijklmnopq
rstuvwxyz

Numbers:
0123456789

NEW

Fig. 2:

Autobahn Tomatica

Uppercase:
ABCDEFGHIJKLMN
OPQRSTUVWXYZ

Lowercase:
abcdefghijklmnopq
rstuvwxyz

Numbers:
0123456789

NEW

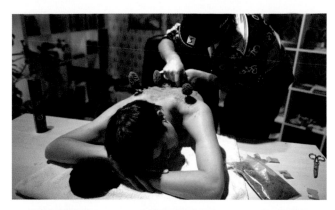

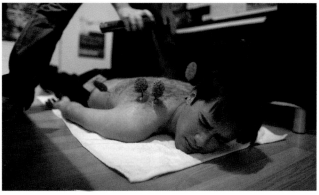

Freshfonts
Autobahn

Left: *Freshfonts* sprang from an invitation to do a Pecha Kucha presentation (where 20 slides are presented for 20 seconds each). Autobahn decided to launch a new project specifically for this talk. Inspired by the limited amount of time available, the team started by writing with tools not usually used for writing. The original idea was to generate a less legible font using gravity. Toothpaste, tomato ketchup and hair gel turned out to be the

best resources. These materials determined the shapes, and with that the character, of the final letters. Because of its neutral appearance, Helvetica was used as a blueprint. The fonts Gelvetica, Heldentica and Tomatica were the result.

Verkenners
Autobahn

This page, top: Autobahn created a book for their client Verkenners, who focus on collaborations between artists and area developers. The image concept

for their publication was inspired by Levi of Veluw's photo series *Landscapes*. In consultation with Levi, Autobahn used this image to create a typographic visual. Photos: Marieke Wijntjes.

Tapewriter
Autobahn

This page, bottom: *Tapewriter* was one of Autobahn's first type experiments: a font based on the grid of a football cage and the width of a roll of duct tape. The idea behind the font is that anyone in possession of a roll of

tape can submit his or her message to the world. Tapewriter was developed during a seminar at Utrecht School of the Arts (HKU) with Richard van de Laken and Eric Wie, and was later developed into a type specimen.

A 35

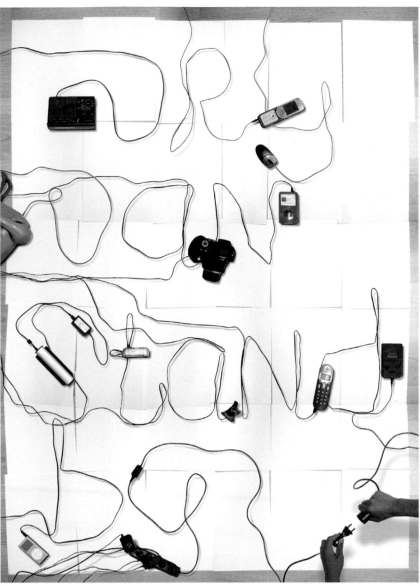

Utrecht Uitfeest Leidsche Rijn
Autobahn
Left: Autobahn created the award-winning concept and graphic design for the typographic routing (huge wayfinding sculptures) of the first Utrecht Uitfeest Leidsche Rijn. This was a series of cultural acts and music performances, based around 25 works of art, organized by the City of Utrecht and Beyond, the permanent art program of Leidsche Rijn in the Netherlands. The location of the event was relatively new and unexplored, so a particularly clear and visible signage was required. Autobahn developed architectural typographic objects, laser-cut out of sustainable polystyrene. The immediate impact of the big white numbers in the landscape ensured that visitors found their way. Autobahn also designed the identity and several products for the event, including the programme, flyers, posters and banners and maps.

NRC Next magazine
Autobahn
Above: Autobahn was asked by *NRC Next* magazine to illustrate a series of articles typographically. This assignment resulted in vector illustrations and photographic solutions, and ultimately a silver European Design Award in the Book & Editorial Illustration category in 2009. *'Het gras van de buren...'* ('The Neighbour's Grass...') was an article about envy and how begrudging other people's happiness will eventually cause our own downfall. The article *'Vrij van stand-by'* ('Free of Stand-by') was about saving energy by pressing the 'off' button. *'Ja, schat...'* ('Yes, dear...') gives an insight into manipulation in relationships. *'Bang voor de knal'* ('Afraid of the Bang') was an article about a woman who was too scared to drive after a car accident with a child.

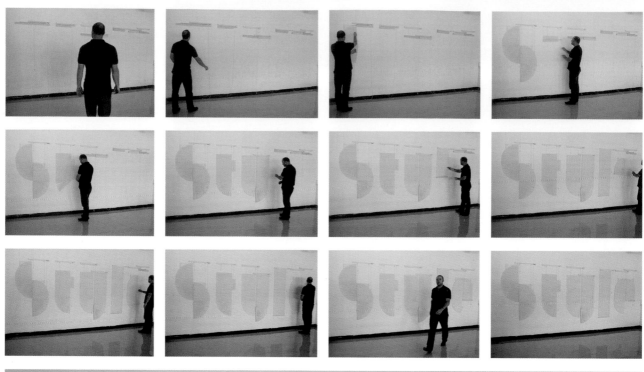

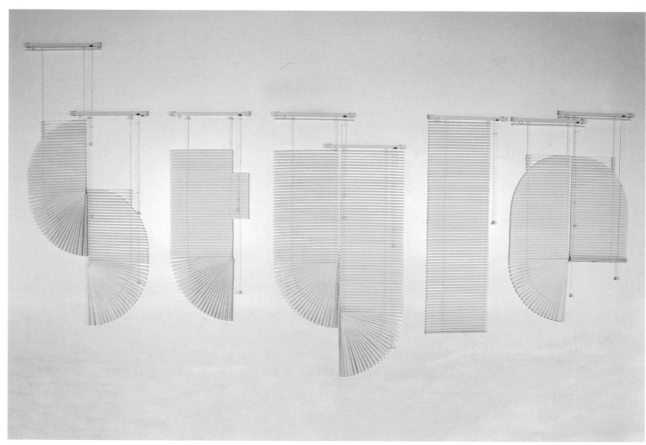

abcdefghijklmnopqr
stuvwxyz   venetian
closed   regular   open

abcdefghijklm asifa
nopqrstuvwxyz

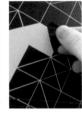

Venetian

Andrew Byrom

Left: Liverpool-born, Los Angeles-based graphic designer, teacher and 3D type specialist Andrew Byrom created *Venetian* in 2008 – a stencil typeface design commissioned by *Elle Decoration* magazine (UK). It was inspired by the forms created when opening and closing a venetian blind.

St. Louis/ASIFA

Andrew Byrom

This page, top: Shown here are polished plastic trophies that were commissioned by ASIFA-Hollywood – a society of animators working to preserve and celebrate historical and contemporary animation. The trophies are for their animation competition winners. The logo and typeface were designed to work for print, digital animation and for the trophies. The logo and trophies use Andrew's stencil typeface *St Louis*, from 2008.

TSS²

Andrew Byrom

This page, bottom: *TSS²* from 2008 is a proposal for a low-cost temporary signage system. It is fabricated from corrugated plastic with peel-off segments to reveal a white background that enables every letter (upper- and lowercase) and number to be constructed. The design, which is lightweight and flat-packed, is intended for indoor or outdoor use in shops, cafés, conferences and gallery openings.

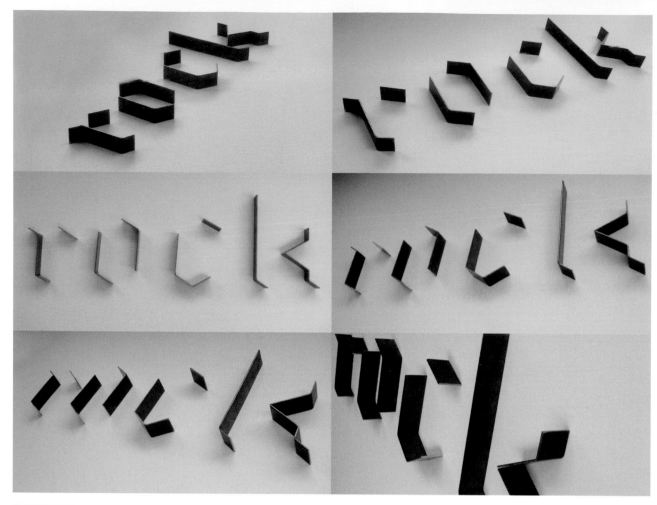

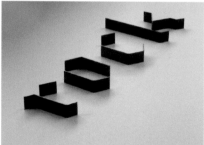

abcdefghij
klnmopqr
stuvwxyz

st.julian

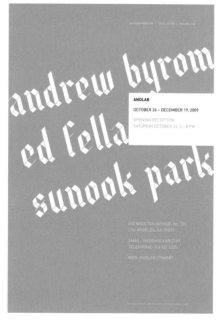

andrew byrom
ed fella
sunook park

the everyday world
is invisible
until we are forced to see it
differently ...

art is a primary means of making
strange the already seen,
already known

victor shklovsky, 1918

abcdefghijklmnopqrstuvwxyz
abcdefghijklmnopqrstuvwxyz
1234567890

bloodclot

St. Julian
Andrew Byrom
Left, top: *St. Julian*, from 2010, is a 2D/3D stencil design influenced by historical German black-letter designs. The 3D signage, fabricated in ⅛-inch steel, comes in and out of view as it is passed. The 2D version was created for a poster announcing an exhibition of the typographic works of Andrew Byrom, Ed Fella and Sunook Park at the ANDLAB Gallery, Los Angeles, in 2009.

Type-Step
Andrew Byrom
Left, bottom: *Type-Step* from 2008 is a design for typographic concrete stepping-stones.

Fresh
Andrew Byrom
This page, left: Andrew designed his first typeface while studying at the University of East London in 1994. This simple design was called *Fresh* and, like most of his work since, it was based on a three-dimensional object: in this case, a bendy straw.

Bloodclot
Andrew Byrom
This page, right: The original *Bloodclot* design from 1996 was a digital typeface that was inspired by the shapes found in sticking plasters. Andrew took the forms found in these everyday objects as a starting point and developed them into a full character set (uppercase, lowercase, numbers and so on). The *Bloodclot* design was revisited in 2008 and a physical handmade version was produced by placing plasters (collected from different brands) directly onto the page to create 26 letters/low-relief objects.

Interiors Light
Andrew Byrom

Left: The initial concept for *Interiors Light* was inspired by Marcel Breuer's Wassily Chair. It was simply intended to be a rounded chrome tubular steel version of the original Interiors design (shown above). As the project developed in 2005, Byrom began to realize that by thinking on a smaller scale each letter could be constructed in neon. The limitations of working in neon were tough on the original concept. He reworked the design several times and began to embrace the constraints of this beautiful and delicate material.

Interiors
Andrew Byrom

Above: *Interiors* was originally conceived as a digital font in 2003. It was inspired by an old wooden chair in the corner of Byrom's London office, which, when looked at from a certain angle, resembled the letter h. Using the three-dimensional principles of this simple form, and closely adhering to type design conventions, 26 letters of the alphabet were drawn and generated as a font. They were later constructed in three dimensions using tubular steel into full-scale furniture frames. Because the underlying design concept is typographical, the end result becomes almost freestyle furniture design. Letters like m, n, o, b and h can be viewed as simple tables and chairs, but other letters, like e, g, a, s, t, v, x and z, become beautiful abstract pieces of furniture.

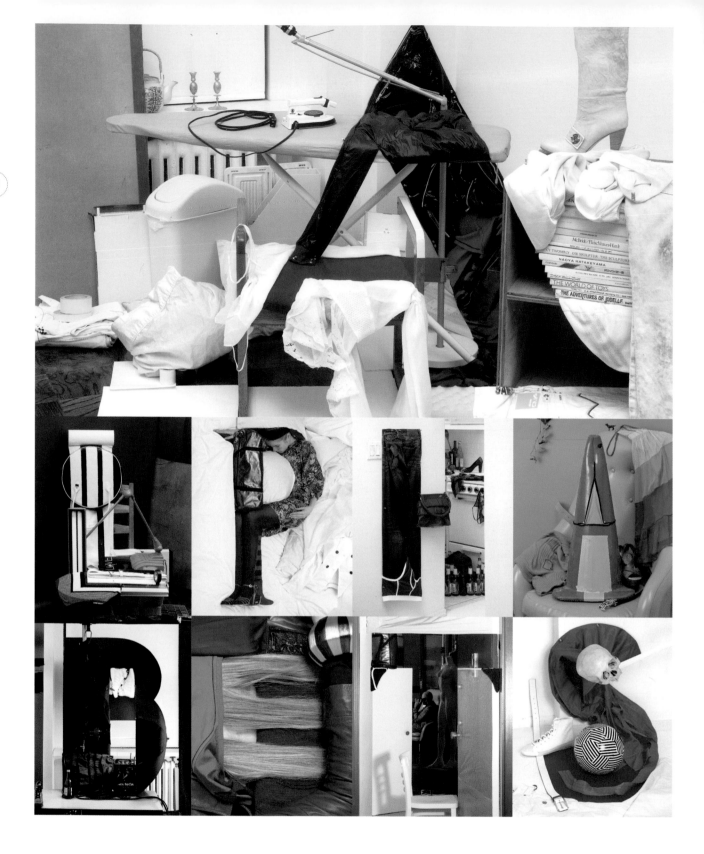

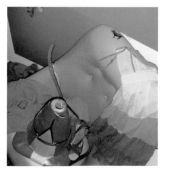

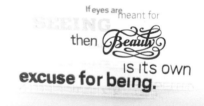

Alphabets

Bela Borsodi

Left: Austrian photographer Bela Borsodi is based in New York. He shot this series, entitled *Alphabets*, in 2009 for French *WAD* magazine #39. Every artist was given a letter to work with, and Bela's letter was 'A'. Bela decided to take this theme quite literally and to spell out the word 'Alphabets' in his apartment using clothes and random objects. He also appears with his girlfriend in some of the pictures. The stylist working with him on

this project was Akari Endo-Gaut. This photographic series allowed him to revise and refine an idea that he had worked on with Stefan Sagmeister in 2003 that also involved typography – readable only from one 'correct' position (see page 197).

5th Typophile Film Festival

Brent Barson

Above: Creative director Brent Barson is assistant professor in Brigham Young University's graphic design department in Provo, Utah, USA. He has

created the opening titles for a variety of independent films, including all the motion graphics for the Typophile Film Festival. For the fifth festival, Brent and his students were commissioned to create opening titles that properly introduced and branded the festival – open to anything relevant to typography, motion graphics, design history or type design. A few of the final stills are shown above; results of a visual typographic feast about the five senses, and how they contribute to and enhance our

creativity. Everything in the film is real; no computer-generated effects were used. The challenges that were faced by those involved in creating the 2009 titles included learning the ins and outs of laser-cutting and dealing with the structural characteristics of Jello and squash ... both are very fragile.

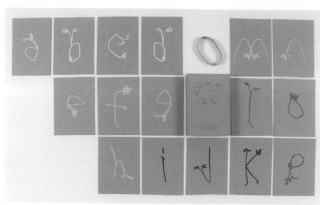

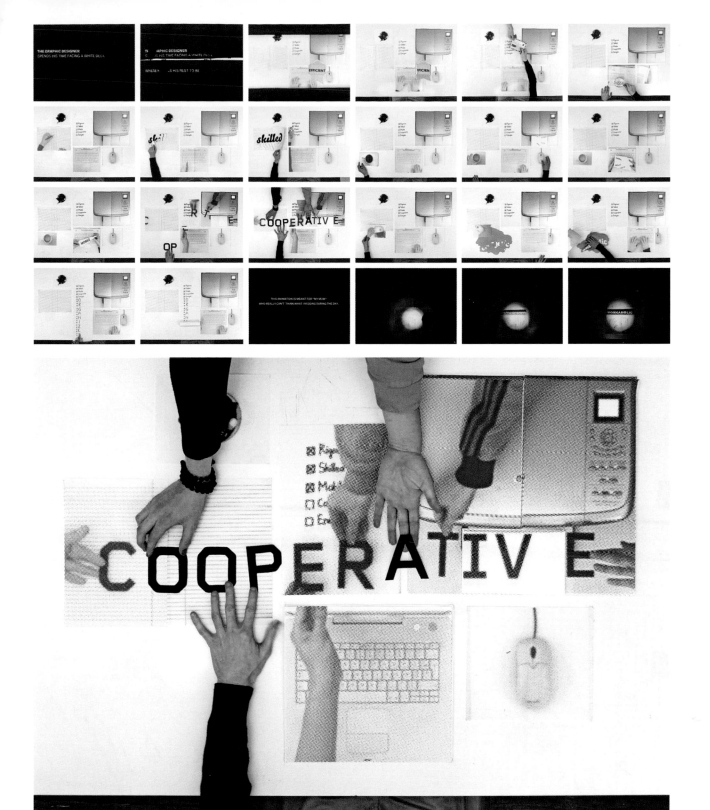

Cress Paper
Bola Cooper
Left, top: UK-based graphic designer and illustrator Bola Cooper created the *Cress Paper* project based on the idea that she could recycle the free newspapers that are handed out around London to passers-by. She decided to turn the paper waste into handmade paper that could then be used to grow cress. Bola produced a book featuring (besides other things) how many sheets of paper she could make from each newspaper. She also made a typeface from the cress seeds that she grew on the paper. Bola used the cress she harvested to form the alphabet and numbers, and then screenprinted the typeface onto board cards with colours that resemble the various colours seen on a cress shoot.

Instruction/Construction
Bradley–McQuade collaboration
Left, bottom: Thom Bradley and Jamie McQuade were in their final year studying graphic design at Kingston University in the UK when they submitted their work to this book. The team had already collaborated several times before, including their work on the *Instruction/Construction* brief, which asked them to *'create and implement a form of typographic code/coding system in the form of a poster'*. The poster starts life whole, in one piece, with a series of horizontal facing lines, either solid or hatched. Following the poster's instructions, one can then create folded letters.

The White Desk
Benoit Lemoine and Cécile Boche
Above: Benoit Lemoine and Cécile Boche created this very cleverly executed stop-frame animation through a sequence of interactions between two scenes playing on two levels. On one hand, there are the printed objects and, on the other, the character sitting at the desk.

Classe préparatoire
aux examens d'entrée
des écoles d'art,
des mises à niveau
d'arts appliqués,
des écoles d'architecture.

Ecole municipale
des Beaux-Arts
Centre Charner
22000 Saint-Brieuc

Téléphone : 0296625521
Fax : 0296043715
beaux-arts3@wanadoo.fr
www.prepa-art-bretagne.fr

Saint-Brieuc

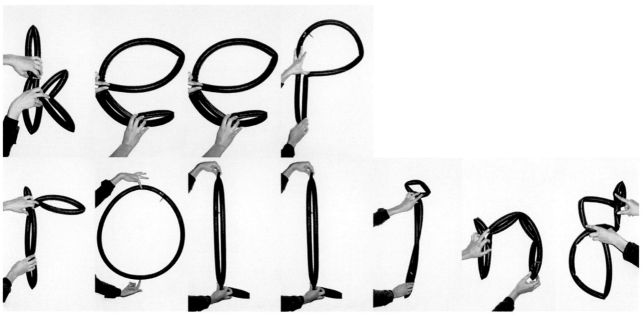

Prépa écoles d'art
Benoit Lemoine
Left, top: French graphic designer Benoit Lemoine studied in Belgium before moving to Rotterdam in the Netherlands. He created *Prépa écoles d'art* for the Beaux-Arts de Saint-Brieuc in France. This visual was used for a poster and flyer announcing the foundation class of the entrance exams to the applied art and architecture schools. The type was created with superimposed coloured paper sheets.

Drink
Benoit Lemoine
Left, bottom: In 2007, Benoit Lemoine designed the *Drink* installation for a contemporary art space. The three-dimensional letters were contained in a pyramid of plastic cups.

Pneuma
BANK
This page, top: Berlin-based design studio BANK was founded by French/German duo Laure Boer and Sebastian Bissinger. They created the *Pneuma* typeface in 2007, while the Keep Rolling lettering was used for a 2008 New Year's card.

Soap magazine
BANK
This page, bottom: The logo and proposed masthead for *Soap* magazine was designed in 2007. The sample cover (detail, top of cover) shows BANK's foam logo in action. All headlines throughout the magazine were also supposed to be set in this foam type, superimposed on the layout and visuals.

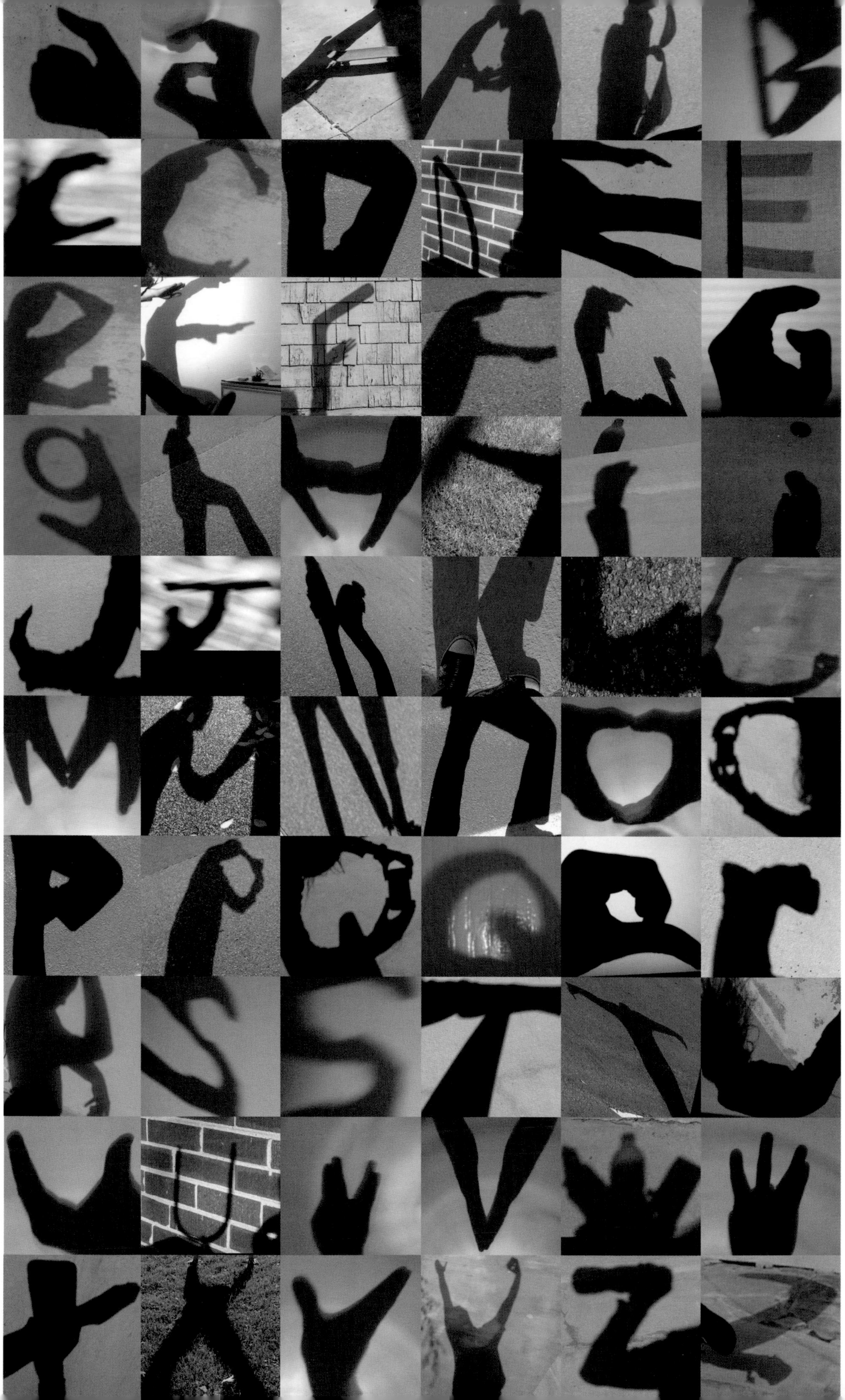

Shadow Alphabet
Cheil USA
Left: The Wow Challenges are a global campaign from Samsung Mobile created by Cheil USA. Found online and hosted by internet personality Ze Frank, the campaign presents participants with three consecutive challenges. Anyone in the world can participate in these, with any mobile phone. All this fun supports two great causes: Architecture for Humanity and The Nature Conservancy. The voting community determines which charity receives a greater percentage of a $30,000 donation from Samsung Mobile. Challenge 1: Use your shadow to make three-dimensional letters, capture them with your mobile, upload them and help create the *Shadow Alphabet*. Then use the shadow letters to write a message and tell the world just what gives you a charge out of life. Online performance artist & internet personality: Ze Frank; senior art director: Kelly Shoemaker; senior copywriter: Brian Gield; junior art director: Soo Bak; design technologist: Phil Ramunno; program manager: Nicole Fiandaca; engagement directors: Jed Michaelson & Shawn Kim; creative director: Ann Marie Mathis; executive creative director: Timothy Bruns.

CR subscriptions page
Craig Ward
Above: New York-based Craig Ward is a typographer and designer who likes playing with words. He was commissioned by *Creative Review* magazine in 2009 to create a visual for their subscriptions page following the theme *'Make Creative Review a part of your world'*. Inspired by the work of pioneering artist Felice Varini, this piece was created using fluorescent tape.

BADOD TYPOGR GRAAPHY IS IS EVERYSI BLWHERE

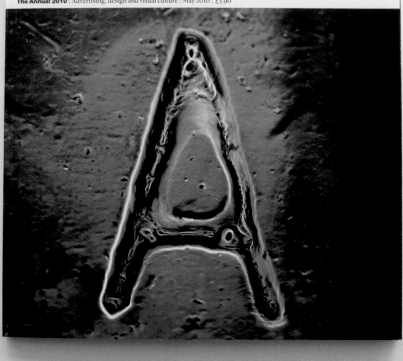

CreativeReview

The Annual 2010 | Advertising, design and visual culture | May 2010 | £5.90

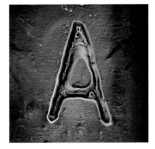

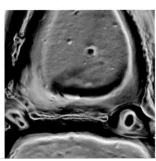

BCUC poster
Craig Ward

Left: Using 7.6 cm (3 in)-high wooden letters on a wall, Craig Ward of Words are Pictures created this self-initiated piece to promote a talk and course he was giving at his former college – Buckinghamshire Chilterns University College, UK.

The Annual cover, 2010
Craig Ward

Above: This image for *Creative Review's The Annual* cover from May 2010 was grown out of pollen cells in an immunology lab. Each year for *The Annual, Creative Review* asks a different person to come up with a cover image based on a capital 'A'. In recent years, this brief has resulted in imagery on an increasingly grand scale. In 2010, however, Craig decided to buck this trend by going much, much smaller and creating some

cell-level typography. Craig approached a couple of UK universities with his idea and discovered that making letterforms from cells was possible, if a little costly (he was quoted anything up to £250,000). But he persevered and was eventually put in touch with Frank Conrad, *'a friend of a friend,'* he says, *'who happened to be an immunologist at the University of Denver'* (the lab shown above). After many experiments in the lab, the final visual was ready; the cover was

printed using a metallic base ink to bring out the details. Concept and art direction: Craig Ward of Words are Pictures; photos and cell manipulation: Frank Conrad, with lab assistance from Bastion Ridley; *Creative Review's* magazine art director: Paul Pensom.

More *Annual* covers can be seen on page 164.

CRAIG WARD &
SEAN FREEMAN &
ALISON CARMICHAEL

Photos: Sean Freeman and
Mark Sinclair.

If You Could Collaborate

**Craig Ward, Sean Freeman and
Alison Carmichael**

If You Could Collaborate was the
fourth annual 'If You Could'
exhibition, which aims to provide
a platform for the finest creatives
from all over the world to
question their conventional
working methods and outcomes.
The contributors were challenged
to produce something a little
unexpected, by working with
partners of their choosing from
any discipline, profession or
background. There was no brief
to answer, or format to honour –
the only limit was the enterprise
and imagination of the artists
involved, and a liberal 12-month
deadline. Craig Ward teamed up
with fellow type nuts Sean
Freeman and Alison Carmichael
to create a triptych of
approximately 1m (39 in)-high
laser-cut wood pieces inspired by
graffiti they had seen. This
exhibition took place in A
Foundation Gallery at Rochelle
School, London, in January 2010,
and was curated by Alex Bec and
Will Hudson (aka It's Nice That).

&
Conor & David
Left: This self-initiated
typographic poster from 2006,
by Conor Nolan and David Wall
of Dublin-based design studio
Conor & David, celebrates the
form of the ampersand.

You Blow Me Away
Craig Ward
Above: Craig Ward collaborated
with photographer Jason Tozer to
create this self-initiated piece in
2009. *You Blow Me Away* was
screenprinted onto 7 mm (¼ in)
glass before a black pool ball
was thrown through the glass.
The images, while at once kinetic
and exciting, are also studies in
the boundaries of legibility,
as the team managed to capture
the glass at various stages
of destruction.

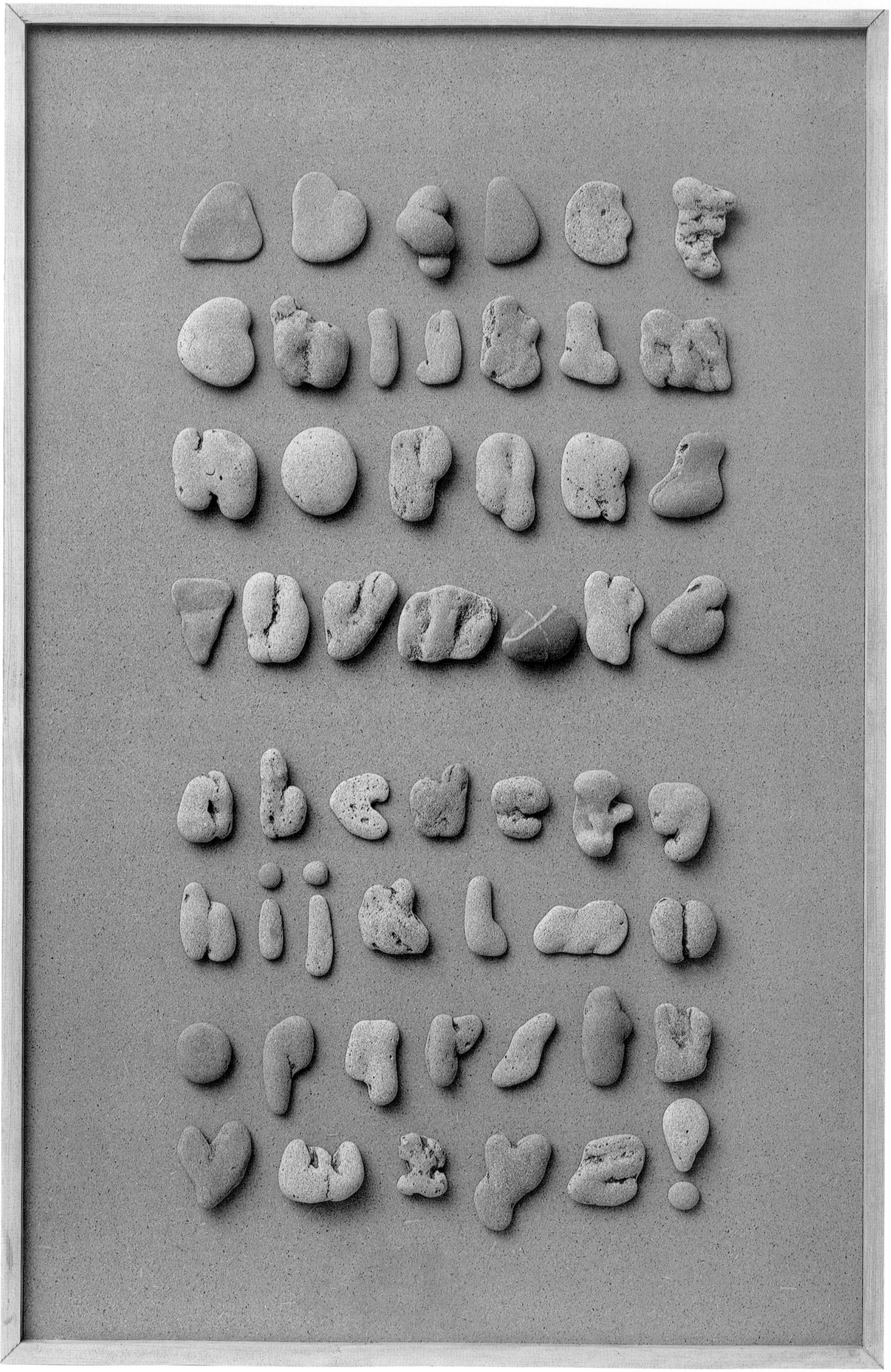

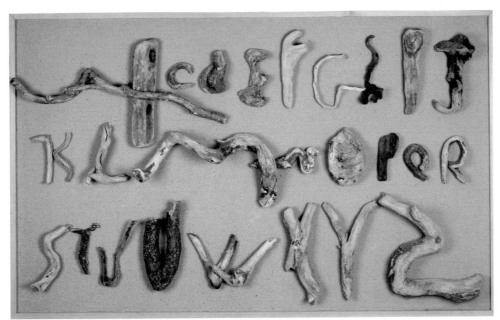

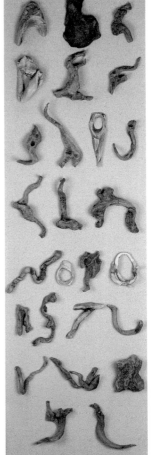

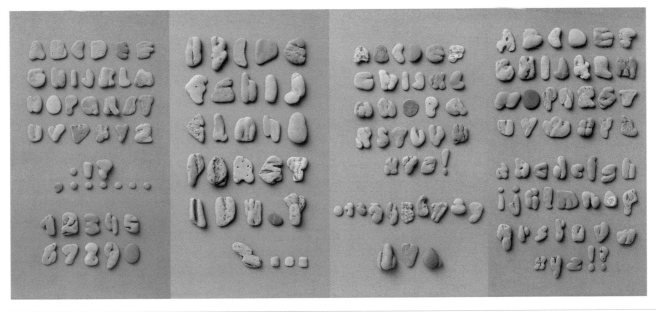

Pebbles and More

Clotilde Olyff

In 2010, Brussels-based graphic designer, typographer, author and teacher Clotilde Olyff celebrated 20 years of collecting alphabets from French beaches. She now has over 30 complete alphabets in pebbles (uppercase, lowercase, numbers and punctuation). There was one interruption of approximately two years: an oil tanker ran aground in northern Spain and polluted all the beaches of southwestern France. The beaches have since been cleaned to remove all the spilled oil, but unfortunately this cleaning process also took away all the shells and stones. The tide and the violence of the waves have brought some of them back now, but Clotilde finds fewer examples. While waiting for the pebbles to return, she has discovered alphabets from pieces of wood and waste brought in by the sea. *'Pebbles are like wine: there are good and bad years, depending on the moods of the Atlantic Ocean!'* Photos: Fabien de Cugnac.

FOAM Album 07

Corriette Schoenaerts

Left, top: For the cover of the *FOAM Album 07* – a 2007 review of the Amsterdam Museum of Photography (FOAM), Amsterdam-based Belgian photographer Corriette Schoenaerts manually cut the numbers 0 and 7 out of all the pictures that were to be printed in the book. The results were two piles of around 500 pictures each. At the top and bottom of these piles, Corriette put two images taken in the museum

itself, literally cutting through the museum's 2007 activities and putting them back into their exhibition space, which the book reflects.

Alpha Bread

Clotilde Olyff

Left, bottom: Alpha Bread was an edible type experiment carried out by Brussels-based graphic designer, author and teacher Clotilde Olyff.

XYZ: Spatial Typography

Chris Tozer

Above: Fascinated by the possibilities of typography as image, London-based graphic designer Chris Tozer began experimenting with three-dimensional type during the final year of his graphic design degree at University College Falmouth, UK. He created a series of type experiments that led to a book called *XYZ: Spatial Typography* documenting the results in 2007. Shown here are some of the many gems.

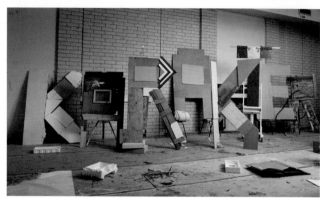

COLOUR 30 03 04   LUNA KRUGER
FOTO CORRISTTE SCHOENAERTS
TYPEFACE JULIA BORN

WWW.QUARANTINE.NL

QUARANTINE SERIES   OFF THE
                           WALL
TUE 30 MARCH 2004   20 30 HRS

FILMS BY YANG FUDONG

                    FINALIST
              HUGO BOSS PRIZE
URBAN LOVE STORIES AND THE
ALIENATED LIVES OF THE
NEW CHINESE MIDDLE CLASS

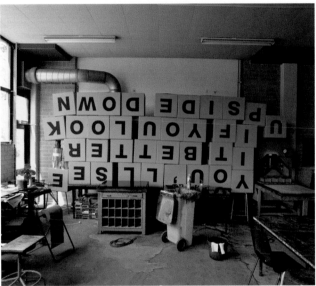

Qualities Needed
Corriette Schoenaerts
Left, top: Photographer Coriette Schoenaerts, in collaboration with 178 Aardige Ontwerpers, created a series of visuals for Utrecht School of the Arts (HKU). For this campaign, qualities deemed necessary to succeed as an artist were determined. A future student would either have these qualities, or be willing to develop them during their education. Illustrated qualities included imagination, character, dedication, boldness,

passion, ambition, ideas, fun and talent.

Quicker
Corriette Schoenaerts
Left, bottom, left: Commissioned by ad agency Addison NY and art directed by Jason Miller, Coriette created this visual for American paper manufacturer Neenah Paper in 2009.

Quarantine Yang Fudong invite
Corriette Schoenaerts
Left, bottom, right: Featuring folded paper letters, this invitation for the Quarantine Art Space, announcing 'Off the Wall', an exhibition by Yang Fudong, was created by Corriette together with Julia Born and Luna Maurer.

Quotes
Corriette Schoenaerts
Above: Corriette in collaboration with De Designpolitie created these pictures as part of a 2005 marketing campaign for Utrecht

School of the Arts (HKU). Quotations by world-famous personalities painted on big cardboard cubes reflect the ambitions of both the school itself and its (future) students. At the same time, these pictures try to create an impression of the diversity of the School's buildings.

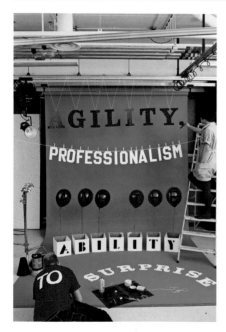

defined by what we refuse to destroy.

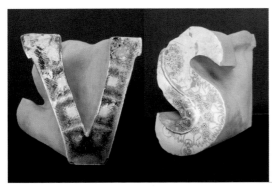

Sheffield Institute of Arts prospectus

Chris Wilkinson

Left: Chris Wilkinson is a graphic designer based in Sheffield, UK. Since around 2007, Chris has developed a passion for creating 3D type and was lucky enough to be able to use it in a few projects including this extraordinary series created for the Sheffield Institute of Arts prospectus 2010. Photography: Tom Jackson. Workshop assistance: Ian Broome (Sheffield Hallam University) and Lucia Kempsey.

Defined. Walnut Woodtype

Charlie Hocking

This page, top: Multi-disciplinary graphic designer Charlie Hocking is based in London. The original concept behind this typeface, made from walnut wood, was to create something that almost looked alive; something that was organic in its form and that would reflect the environmental message attached to a new branding campaign that this was a part of. Making the letterforms three-dimensional heightens the fluidity of the typeface, letting the viewer imagine the forms taking on a life of their own.

Ceramics

Charlotte Cornaton

This page, bottom: Freelance graphic designer, videographer and ceramicist Charlotte Cornaton graduated in art direction and graphic design from ESAG Penninghen in Paris in 2009, and has also attended ceramics courses at Central Saint Martins in London. She continues to develop the work that she started with her complex final-year project, *Vanitas*, by mixing 3D design in ceramics and graphic design with stop-motion video. Shown here are ceramics made from moulds, following preparatory work in plaster, using profile and template. *Versus*: earthenware silkscreened with scientific engraving. *Ceramic*: matter interferes with the letters, printed from lace, plastic, bubble wrap and other materials.

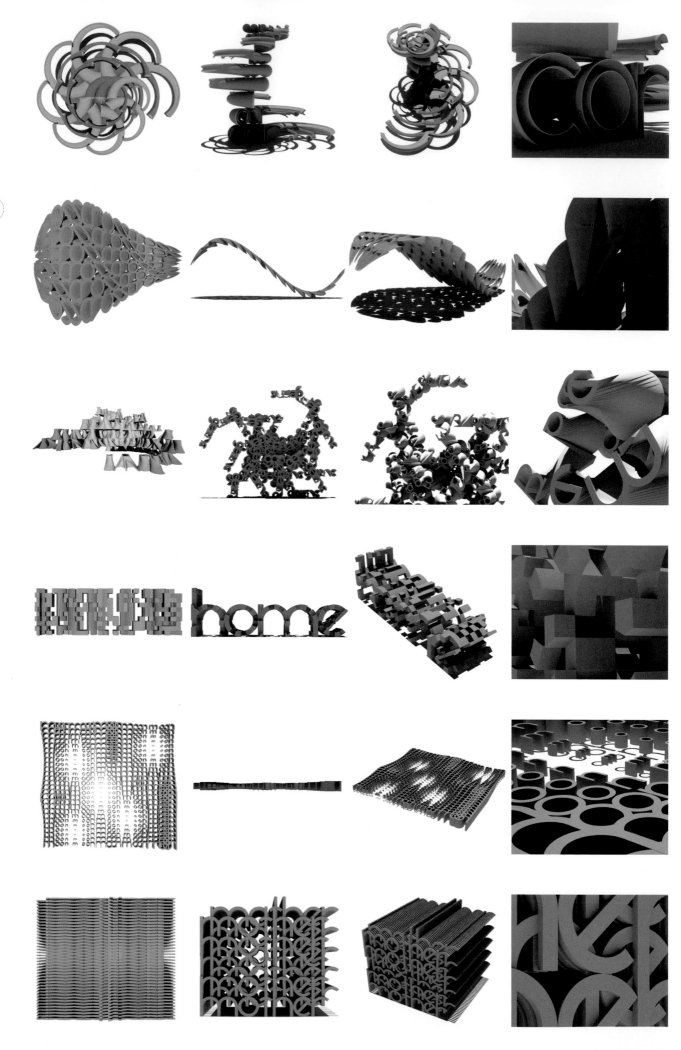

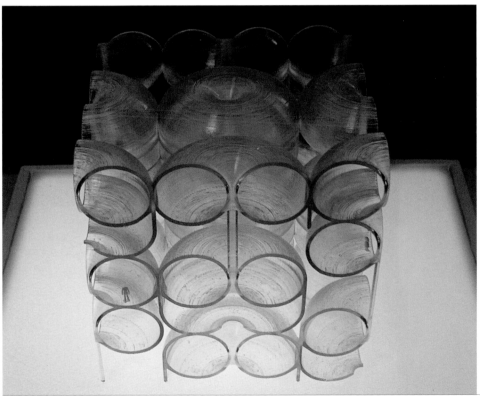

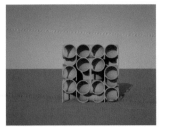

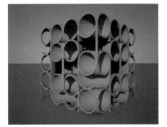

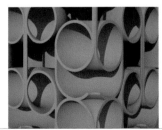

Typotectonics

Chrysostomos Tsimourdagkas

Chrysostomos Tsimourdagkas is a registered architect in Greece. He has worked as a graphic, industrial and architectural designer for several firms including Zaha Hadid Architects. When this book was being compiled, he was pursuing a PhD at the Department of Architecture of the Royal College of Art in London, investigating ways in which typography can be incorporated into the architectural field. What fascinates him is the blending of the boundaries between typography and architecture, (which he calls 'typotecture'), for the generation of spaces that are at the same time functional and communicative. The digital images shown on the left are part of an experiment in creating an application capable of generating a variety of 3D letterforms with potential architectural applications, which Chrysostomos describes as 'typotectonics'. The user, after selecting a typeface, will be able to create three-dimensional components by parametrically extruding the glyphs through the definition of a certain set of critical values such as path, curving, scaling, twisting and style of extrusion. The next step, after selecting a word, is to define a second parametric operation, such as arraying, tiling, branching or spiralling, in order to aggregate the three-dimensional components of that word and generate the final form. Eventually, the user will be able to export that form and further manipulate it according to given needs. Above: Digital and physical models of two typographical sculptures.

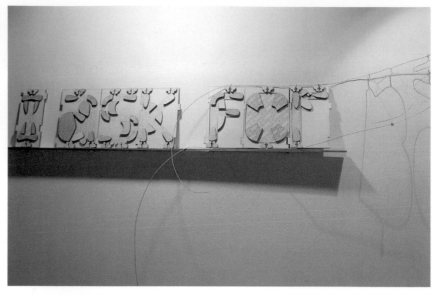

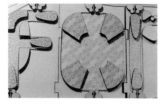

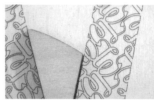

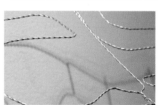

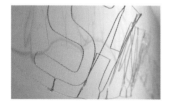

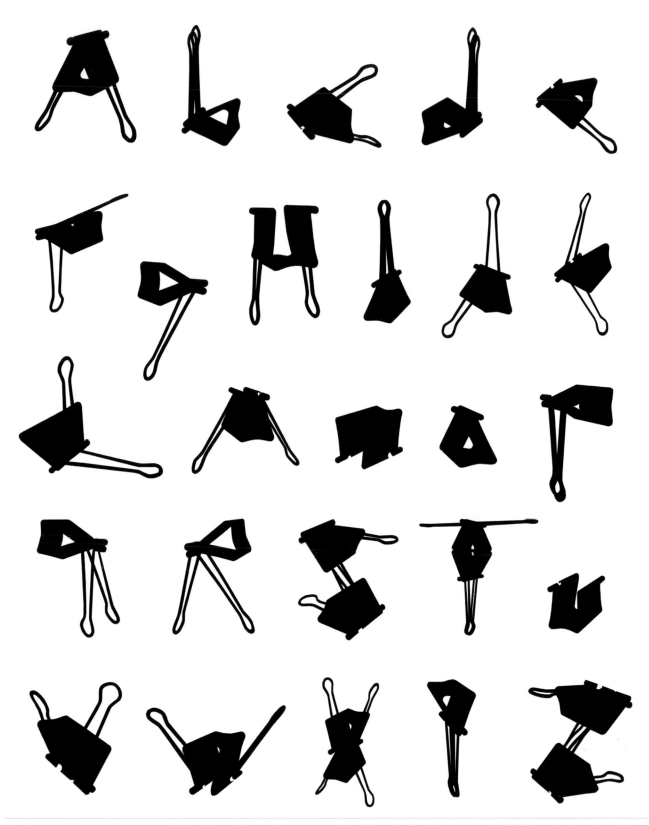

Prototype

Denise Gonzales Crisp

Left, top: Denise Gonzales Crisp is professor of graphic design at North Carolina State University, and designer of the occasional studio SuperStove!. She was invited by curators Jimmy Luu and Ryan Molloy to attend the 2009 exhibition 'Dimension+ Typography' at I Space Gallery in Chicago. She constructed *Prototype*, a 'text garland' of twisted copper wire, 25.4 cm x 10 m (10in x 33ft), that meandered through the galleries, using the third and fourth dimensions to give form to the act of reading. The jigs, made of laser-cut basswood, turned out to be more compelling than the garland, and gave Denise a new fascination with tools that make type, now an ongoing project of hers. Photos: Jimmy Luu.

Bloom

Daryl Tanghe

Left, bottom: Graphic designer Daryl Tanghe is based in Seattle, Washington, but grew up in Metro Detroit, where he studied at the College for Creative Studies in Detroit, Michigan. It was at college in his typography class with tutor Chad Reichert that Daryl became interested in three-dimensional type. Flowering plants were used to construct this typeface, *Bloom*, in 2007.

Bulldog

Dave Wood

Above: *Fuse* magazine was being relaunched with an underpinning concept of 'physical interaction'. Following a D&AD student brief, in 2008 London-based graphic designer Dave Wood designed a custom typeface for the magazine made entirely from bulldog clips. The two clips used to create the alphabet were then used to bind the final magazine. This enabled the french-folded pages to be opened and rearranged, allowing new content to be discovered.

ABCDEFGHI
JKLMNOPQ
RSTUVWXYZ
1234567890

PURE RESPECT
LOVE

Gut
Daryl Tanghe
Left, top, left: Like *Bloom* on the previous page, this wooden piece was the result of a college brief: to choose a short word and then illustrate its meaning typographically.

Shredding is all about the details
David Aspinall
Left, top, right: London-based designer David Aspinall created this experimental type piece to explore ways of creating three-dimensional letterforms from two-dimensional materials. The work is made from a large sheet of paper that was manually shredded. Each strip was then folded outwards to create the sentence.

The End
Detail. Design Studio
Left page, bottom: Detail. Design Studio from Dublin was invited with other designers from Ireland and the UK to submit work for a project for Belfast Print Finishers. The theme of the project was 'Finish', and the invited entrants could interpret this in any way they wished. *The End* had a double meaning in this situation that fitted the theme while at the same time being an odd choice for a funeral tribute. Photo: Paul McCarthy.

Made-By campaign
Dolly Rogers
Above: Amsterdam-based agency Dolly Rogers created this alphabet using sustainable clothing. The typeface was used as part of a creative communication strategy for their client Made-By (Solidaridad) and the Sustainable Fashion Week in the Netherlands. The campaign was implemented across television, print and the internet. Photos: Tom Ten Seldam (Studio 5982).

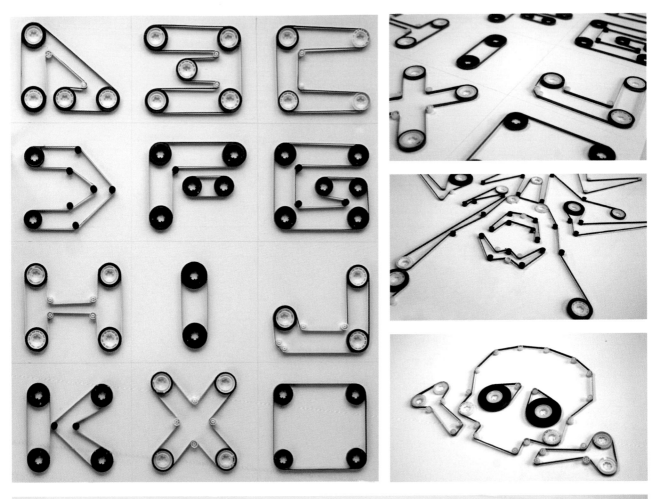

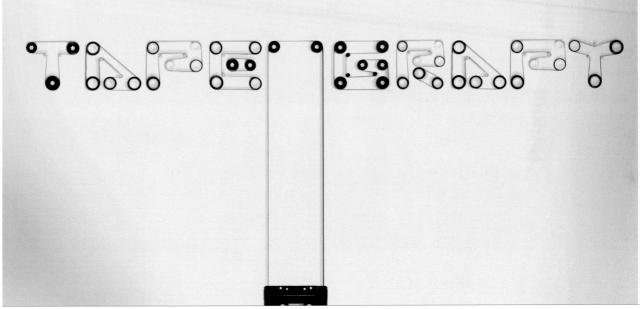

Electronica
Efsun Senturk
Left, top: Originally from Istanbul, Turkey, London College of Communication graduate Efsun Senturk is a freelance graphic designer based in London. She discovered every letter of this alphabet in an electronic card in an amplifier.

Wedi7 Title Sequence
Elfen
Left, bottom: Guto Evans, co-founder of Elfen, a design and branding company based in Cardiff Bay, Wales, art-directed this title sequence created for a general-interest television programme. Commissioned by Tinopolis/S4C, it was shot with 35 mm cameras at the client's location using the settings of their studios, track, lights and rigs. Lead designer: Aaron Easterbrook; camera work and photography: Huw Talfryn and Guto Evans; project manager: Gwion Prydderch.

Tapeography
Ersin Han Ersin
Above: Freelance graphic designer Ersin Han Ersin is based in Ankara, Turkey. He designed *Tapeography* as an homage to the good old cassette tapes he associates with his teenage years and a whole spectrum of emotions. Actually creating the letterforms was a very painstaking and time-consuming process – as everybody who has ever repaired a cassette will be able to attest.

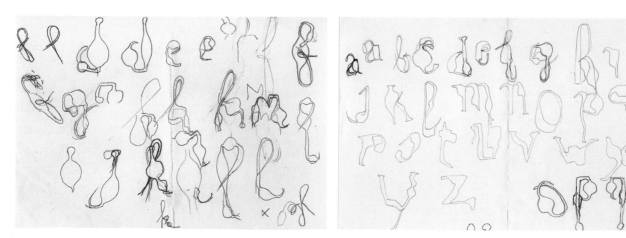

Glass Letterforms

ÉricandMarie

Left: *Glass Letterforms* is a singular project; it is the only 3D type project that design duo Marie and Éric Gaspar has ever worked on. In fact, it is the only typeface they have ever produced. It happened while Marie and Éric, who now live and work in Paris, were still students at the Royal College of Art (RCA) in London. During the first days studying there in 1999, they decided to visit all the workshops that they could find in the RCA building. The most amazing place was the glass workshop. That's when they asked themselves – what kind of shape could be blown in glass? The answer came promptly: letterforms. The medium seemed very appropriate. The liquid glass – still in fusion – reminded them of spoken language, ever moving and fluid. During the process of blowing glass, it rapidly transforms from a liquid to a solid state. When the glass hardens, however, it reminded the designers of written language: structured and definite. To actually create the shapes, Marie and Éric got help from a workshop technician (it takes years to be able to work glass correctly). As glass-blowing is a time-consuming process, they only managed to create ten letterforms, but that was enough for the pair to be happy with the project.

Triangulation

Emeline Brulé

Above: Originally from France, Emeline Brulé moved to Brussels, Belgium, in 2009 to start her studies in visual communication, graphic design and typography at graphic research school ERG. *Triangulation* is a typographic experiment exploring the limits between volumes and flat surfaces and how to combine them. These letters also play with light and shadow.

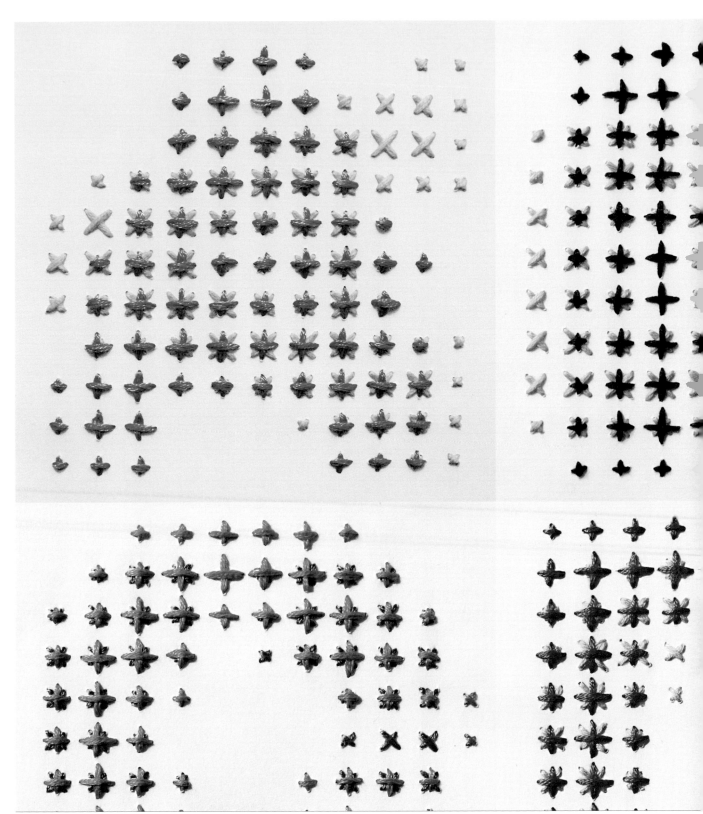

CMYK Alphabet
Evelin Kasikov

Evelin Kasikov is an artist and designer. Born in Estonia, she now lives and works in London. Her work crosses the boundaries between handmade and digital. She creates typographic illustrations by fusing modernist design principles, technology and craft. By transforming printing processes into hand-embroidery, her work is influenced by craft, but still retains the context of graphic design. *CMYK Alphabet* is one of her experiments in craft and design. It is a fusion of tactile and visual perception; the embroidered surface makes the letterforms tactile and three-dimensional, while the overprinted colours blend in the eyes of the viewer. *CMYK Alphabet* consists of 26 sans-serif uppercase letterforms on a 12.7 x 12.7 cm (5 x 5 in) grid. Each letter was hand-embroidered using a combination of two overlapping CMYK colours. The colours were halftoned at 90 and 45 degrees, and these low-resolution screens were then turned into handmade cross-stitch embroidery. The work was created for *UPPERCASE* magazine issue 3, Fall 2009. Evelin was asked to contribute a piece of work for the typography section, but apart from that the brief was open.

Play

Farina Kuklinski

These three-dimensional type experiments by Berlin-based graphic desiger Farina Kuklinski were created while she was studying at the Academie Beeldende Kunsten (Academy of Fine Arts) in Maastricht, the Netherlands, from where she graduated in 2009. The visuals form part of a much larger body of work comprising posters, animations and a book documenting her *Play* project.

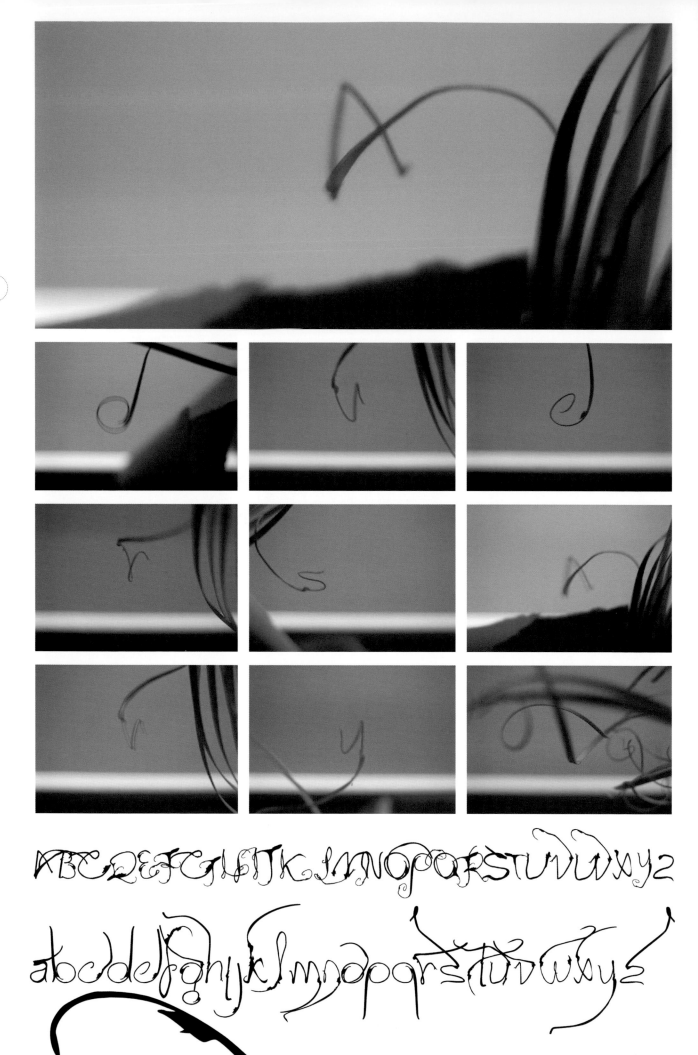

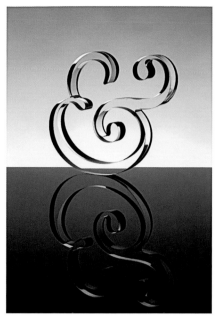
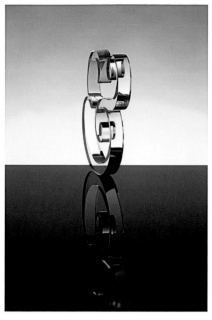

Spring

Ferdinand Alfonso

Left: Ferdinand Alfonso is a graphic designer based in New York City. He created these self-initiated letterforms using a single tendril of scrap paper. He then used the letterforms in a short film that spells out the word 'adversary'. He chose this word as he felt he was fighting with the paper in the process – turning it and flipping it around, trying to get a word out of it. Later he used the letterforms to create a typeface called *Spring*.

29th A&B Awards Identity

Form

Above: In 2007, London-based studio Form were commissioned by Arts & Business (A&B) to create a new identity for the 29th A&B Awards – the UK's most prestigious awards celebrating excellence in the field of business/arts partnerships and sponsorship. With a modern, young and innovative feel in mind, the Form team produced a Perspex model of the A&B ampersand. With the collaboration of photographer

Lee Funnell, they created a series of beautiful still-life shots with the ampersand as 'hero'. Bold typographic layouts accompanied the imagery, and gloss finishes with foil blocking added a tactile and luxury feel. Art direction and design: Form co-founder Paula Benson; art direction: Andy Harvey and Becky Johnson.

06-14. jun, 2009. Novi Sad   cinemacity.org

Fierce 10
Fluid
Left: Lee Basford, from Birmingham-based design consultancy Fluid, created this visual in collaboration with photographer Jonathan Costello. The Fierce Festival is a performance arts festival attracting more than 300,000 attendees. For its tenth birthday, Fierce were planning something much bigger and the design had to reflect this. Fluid created a physical piece of work that could be photographed with some of

the artists. The burning '10' was constructed out of wood and – due to health and safety precautions – photographed separately. The final image was created in Photoshop using the pictures from the photoshoot.

Cracking ABC
Funda Cevik
This page, top: Funda Cevik is a German-born, Turkish graphic designer who now lives in Edinburgh, where she discovered these letter-shaped cracks in pavements in 2009.

Cinema City
Fajn Hajp Agency
This page, bottom: Filip Bojovic, founder of Fajn Hajp Agency in Novi Sad, Serbia, created this ad for the 2009 Cinema City Film and Media Festival in Novi Sad. Visual identity: Joler Vladan, Filip Bojovic, Katarina Lukic Balazikova; AD&D: Filip Bojovic, Katarina Lukic Balazikova; illustration: Katarina Lukic Balazikova, Marijana Zaric; photos: Darko Novakovic, Srdjan Srdjanov, Jana Katic.

THUS GREW THE TALE OF WONDERLAND
THUS SLOWLY, ONE BY ONE,
ITS QUAINT EVENTS WERE HAMMERED OUT
AND NOW THE TALE IS DONE,
AND HOME WE STEER, A MERRY CREW,
BENEATH THE SETTING SUN.

A verse from, *All in the Golden Afternoon*, Lewis Carroll's
introductory poem in the original "Alice's Adventures in Wonderland".

F

Wonderland

Frost*Design

Inspired by the rich history of Tamarama, Sydney-based Frost*Design created a site-specific typographical artwork for the 2009 'Sculpture by the Sea' exhibition. One hundred and thirty-eight fluorescent orange letters spell out a verse from the poem 'All in the Golden Afternoon' from Lewis Caroll's famous children's book *Alice in Wonderland*. The verse stretches across more than 600 m (650 yd) of the Tamarama beach fence. The sculpture references the controversial theme park Wonderland City, which stretched across the beach over 100 years ago, preventing the public from accessing the beach. Creative direction: Vince Frost; design direction: Bridget Atkinson; senior designer: Sarah Estens; copywriter: Lex Courts; project manager: Annabel Stevens; design intern: Erin Fraser.

Rubber band ball alphabet
FL@33

Left: The British postal service hands out vast numbers of rubber bands every day. We almost always receive our mail wrapped in at least one rubber band, and used to throw most of them away until we discovered rubber band balls. Made – you guessed it – from 100 per cent rubber bands, they grow as you add on new rubber bands. We have five or six rubber-band balls here in the studio, ranging from one 9 cm (3½ in) in diameter to little one-week-old ones just 1.5 cm (½ in) in diameter. Using the largest one we had, we took on the challenge of creating an alphabet, restricting ourselves to using a maximum of three green rubber bands to be added to the red ball.

Tower crane letters
FL@33

This page, top: This visual is the very first FL@33 postcard we produced. The artwork was created in 2000 – even before we officially set up the studio in 2001. The artwork formed part of our research into the beauty of tower cranes, leading to FL@33's award-winning *Trans-form* magazine. *Trans-form* was launched at the Royal College of Art's Masters degree show in summer 2001, where this postcard was offered as a free give-away. The tower cranes really did form letters over the period of approximately six months that we studied them outside our studio windows. The visual above did admittedly involve a bit of Photoshop and later led to *Trans-form* cityscape insects.

FL@33 logo cake
FL@33

This page, bottom: Created using 3 eggs, 150 g (5oz) flour (the same weight as 3 eggs without shells), 150 g (5oz) sugar, 150 g (5oz) butter. Mixed and then baked in a pre-heated oven at 180°C (350°F) for 33 minutes.

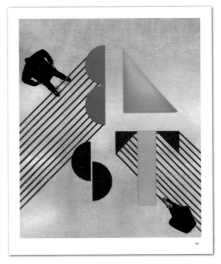

Title 2
Go Welsh

Left, top: Go Welsh is a design studio based in Lancaster, PA, USA. *The Giving Issue,* the second issue of their ongoing promotional project entitled *Title,* was sent prior to the 2008 holiday season. The dimensional letterforms on the cover represent wrapped gifts. Art director: Craig Welsh; designer: Scott Marz.

Earth Will Survive, Will You?
Georgina Potier and Itamar Ferrer

Left, bottom: This is one of many pictures taken as part of a project created by Itamar Ferrer and Georgina Potier in response to an RSA (The Royal Society for the Encouragement of Arts, Manufactures & Commerce) 2008/09 competition brief called 'Elegant Frugality'. A few facts on waste: every year, the UK produces 435 million tonnes of rubbish, or 400 kg (880 lb) per person. Although half the

amount produced by the average American, it is 25 per cent more than that of a French resident. The UK is one of the most wasteful societies in Europe, and its rubbish output is rising by four per cent a year.

Print Magazine Annual
Gluekit

Above: Gluekit is the illustration and design team of Kathleen and Christopher Sleboda. Working from their home studio in Guilford, Connecticut, USA, they created the cover and six interior

spreads for *Print Magazine*'s 2008 Regional Design Annual. Wood, felt, hula hoops, fabric, tape, staples, foam and seams were all employed to create the type throughout the issue. The cover utilized type created out of tape, and previewed some of the three-dimensional forms that were used in the interior type sections. The package was selected by the Type Directors Club for inclusion in *TDC55,* published in 2009.

CREATIVE REVIEW
THE BEST IN VISUAL COMMUNICATION
NOVEMBER 2005 £5.50
A CENTAUR PUBLICATION

CR

SPECIAL
ISSUE
CREATIVE FUTURES

Shining a light on the stars of tomorrow in advertising, graphic design, special effects, animation, typography, illustration, photography, interactive media and commercials direction

"The image of the piece is what is important: it is the process of documentation which turns it into design."
Gareth Holt and Daniel Mair, Creative Futures

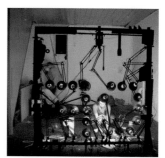

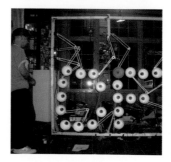

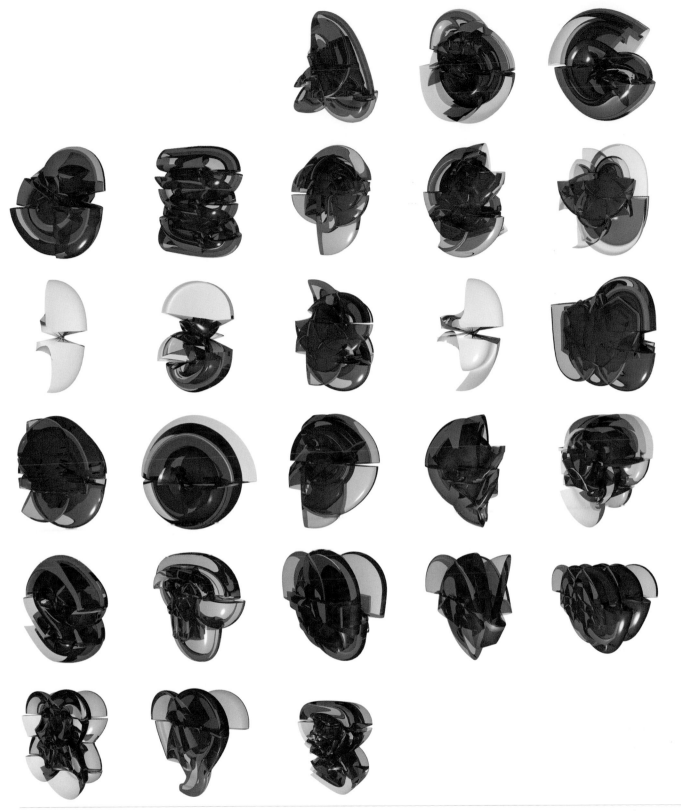

Creative Futures
Gareth Holt
Left: In 2005, London-based designer and art director Gareth Holt collaborated with Daniel Mair and photographer Dan Smith to create this now-classic cover. Commissioned by Nathan Gale – art director at *Creative Review* at the time – this cover design was created following a brief to create a visual that had to convey that it was the Creative Futures Special Issue. Disheartened with the pure digital-generated output of recent times, the decision was to go analogue to create a CF logotype, using 21 anglepoise desk lamps (a much-needed tool for any young designer of the future) to do so. Originally assigned just to design the front cover, the team also managed to get the back cover to feature the back of the installation in order to make sure people knew it was not a Photoshop job.

Incest
Geoff Kaplan
Above: A Jimmy Luu and Ryan Molloy-curated exhibition, 'Dimension+Typography', held in 2009 at the I Space Gallery, Chicago, featured – beside many other projects also included in this book – work by San Francisco-based Geoff Kaplan of General Working Group. Geoff has produced projects for a range of academic and cultural institutions. *Incest* is a series of sleek, translucent shape-shifting letterforms. They are abstracted beyond easy recognition, perhaps only knowable when presented in a chart from A to Z. Around 2008, a few tangible 3D prints of his experimental and often otherwise animated letterforms were produced by Geoff, but were unfortunately never photographed. However, the sculptural qualities are apparent in the stunning visuals shown here.

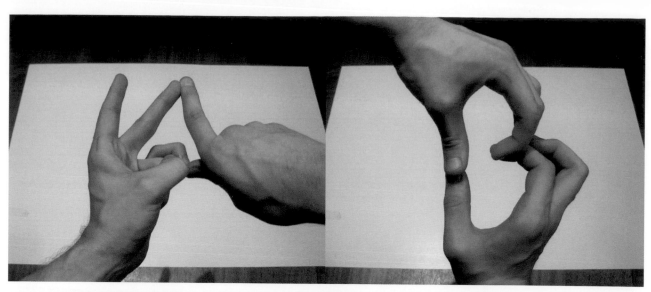

ABCDEEFGHIJKLMNOPQRRSTUUVWYZX

abcdefghijlmnopqrstuvwyz

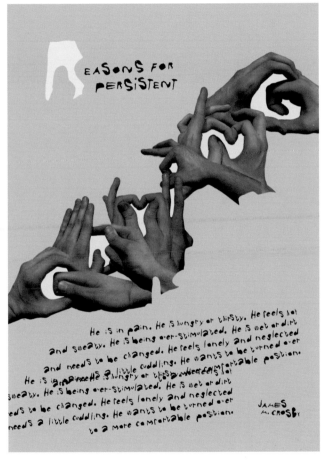

EASONS FOR PERSISTENT

He is in pain. He is hungry or thirsty. He feels hot and sweaty. He is being over-stimulated. He is wet or dirt and needs to be changed. He feels lonely and neglected He is in pain. He is hungry or thirsty. He feels hot sweaty. He is being over-stimulated. He is wet or dirt needs to be changed. He feels lonely and neglected needs a little cuddling. He wants to be turned over to a more comfortable position.

JAMES M. CROSBY

Handwriting

Hijack Your Life

Left and this page, right: Originally from Uppsala, Sweden, Kalle Mattsson (aka Hijack Your Life) now lives and works in Amsterdam, the Netherlands. He created the *Handwriting* alphabet in 2005 as part of a project for Patrick Coppens at the Gerrit Rietveld Academie, Amsterdam. Handwriting was a continuation of the same project that resulted in the *Backbreaker* letters (see page 96). Kalle was watching a film with friends, using a video projector. Before everyone sat down, he was playing around with his hands in the light; instead of creating shadow creatures, he discovered the unusual letters using negative space.

My Beautiful Revolution

Hijack Your Life

This page, left: This record sleeve was created in 2006 for Kalle Mattsson's own band, Caterpillar Ghost. Client: Signature Tunes.

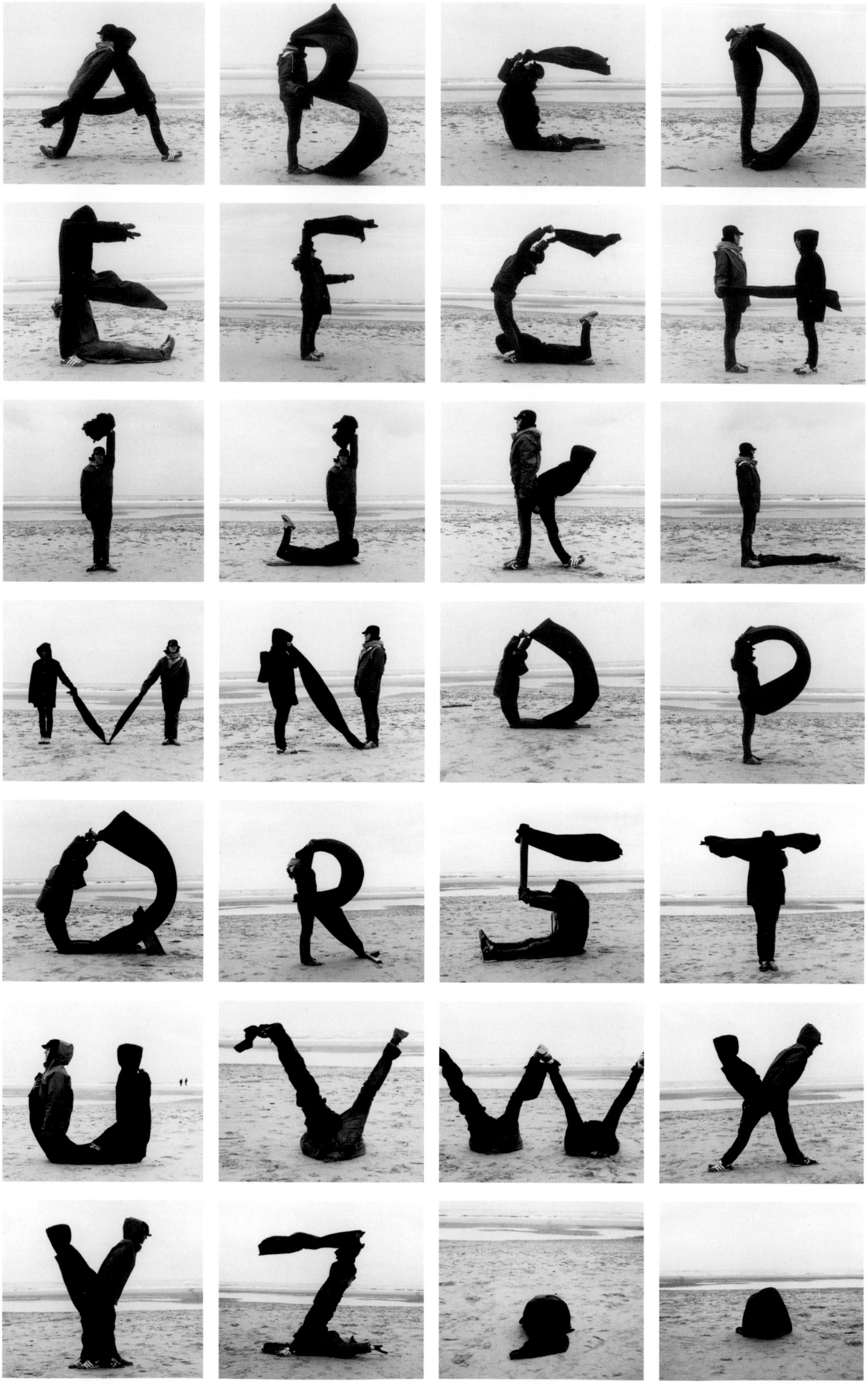

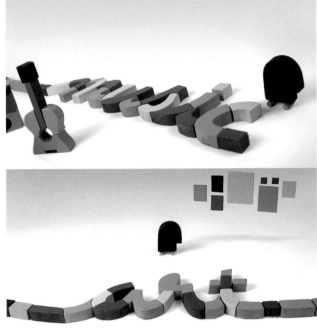

Backbreaker

Hijack Your Life

Left: *Backbreaker* by Kalle Mattsson (aka Hijack Your Life) formed the starting point of a project that later led to his *Handwriting* alphabet (see page 94). Created in 2005 as part of a project for Patrick Coppens at the Gerrit Rietveld Academie, Amsterdam, this project was a collaboration with photographers Monica Tormell and Tomas Adolfs and the model Britta Persson (the second model in the pictures is Kalle himself).

Inspired by an old woodcut typeface featuring letterforms made of people, Kalle started to recreate the idea and to make it his own. He noticed that the P-person had used a sail to create the P, which he liked a lot. Zandvort an Zee, half an hour from Amsterdam, seemed the ideal place to shoot *Backbreaker*. The letters C and D also illustrate the sail idea rather well.

Experimental and Exhibited

HunterGatherer

This page, left: HunterGatherer is a New York City design, illustration, animation and production studio founded by Todd St. John. Shown here are two of Todd's 'Word Boxes', as he calls them, which were created as part of a self-initiated series of wooden sculptures and experimental pieces made between 2002 and 2008.

Swerve Festival Identity

HunterGatherer

This page, right: Commissioned by Flux/Fuel TV in 2007, HunterGatherer developed the overall identity design for Swerve Festival, their environmental design and animations. The designs were created through stop-motions and cut-wood letterforms that recombined into different visuals.

HunterGatherer

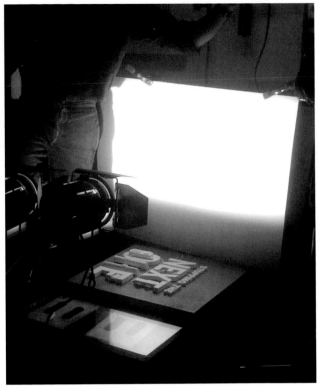

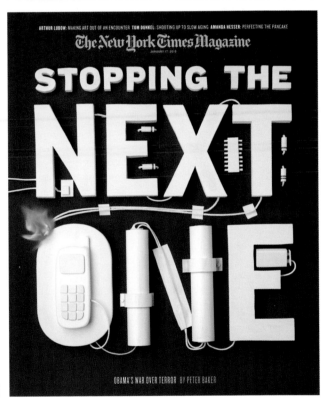

New York magazine cover
HunterGatherer
Left, top: This *New York Magazine* cover from 2009 features an illustration for the 'end of the decade issue' made from painted wood.

HunterGatherer lettering
HunterGatherer
Left, bottom: The company's own name in wood features on their website.

New York Times Magazine cover
HunterGatherer
Above: This commissioned *New York Times Magazine* cover from January 2010 was designed and built by HunterGatherer using cut wood, string and paint. Photos: Andrew Bettles.

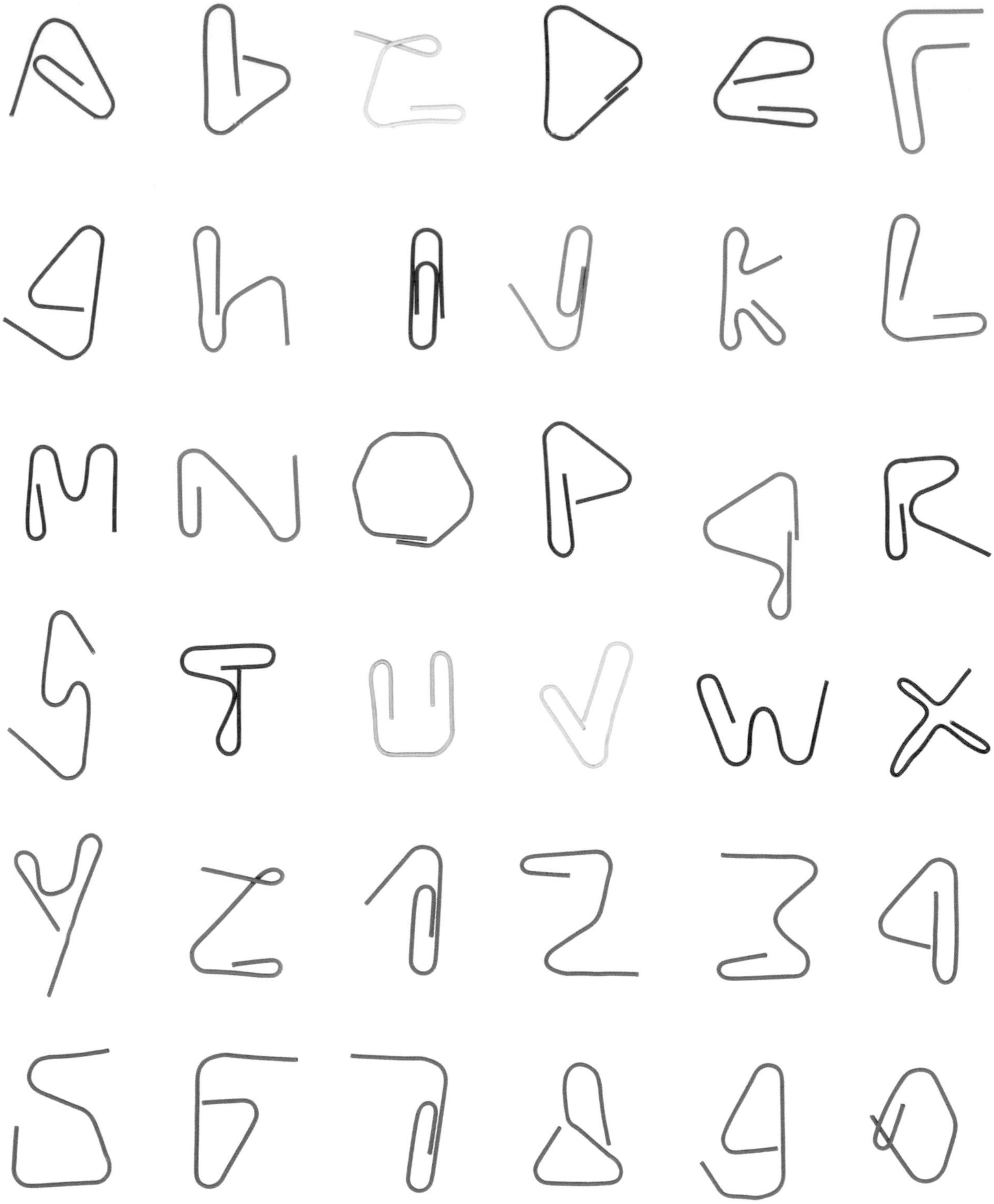

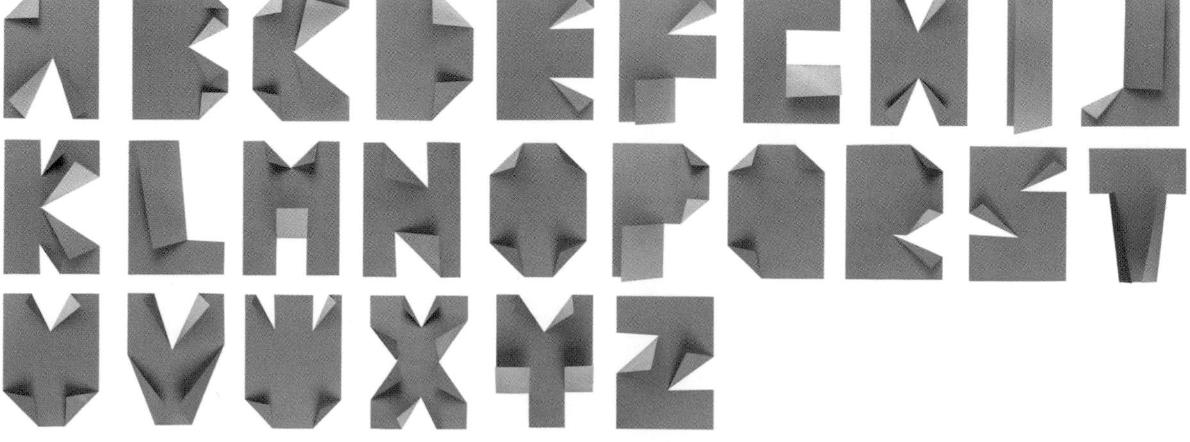

Paperclip and paper typefaces
HandMadeFont
Left: Estonian design company HandMadeFont was founded in 2008 by Vladimir Loginov and Maksim Loginov. They specialize in developing unique and untraditional fonts. Their website, handmadefont.com, offers hundreds of beautifully crafted fonts that can be purchased and used freely for any purpose from business cards to outdoor advertisements. Shown here are two of their many typefaces.

Ogenblik Geduld A.U.B.
Hoax
This page, top: Hoax is a graphic design studio based in Utrecht, the Netherlands. It was founded by Bram Buijs, Steven van der Kaaij and Sven Gerhardt after their graduation from the Utrecht School of the Arts (HKU). The inflatable letters shown here are part of a series of typographic experiments using everyday materials. The idea was to find a way to use the most basic elements of programming, namely on/off. The result was

a series of typographic installations. The materials used were refuse bags, ventilators and tape.

Dox Records' Family Night
Hoax
This page, bottom: Hoax designed these handmade letters for a series of flyers publicizing Dox Records' Family Night, a club night held in Amsterdam's Sugar Factory.

Nike/Produit en Italie
Happycentro
Left, top: Happycentro design studio is based in Verona, Italy. This poster was made for Nike for their 'Produit en Italie' campaign, celebrating the Italian football team that won the 2006 World Cup. It was part of a series based on an old Italian TV show, *Carosello*. Agency: Wieden+Kennedy Amsterdam; creative director: Alvaro Sotomayor; art director: Anders Stake; copywriter: Carlo Cavallone; illustrators: Federico Galvani and Giuliano Garonzi; producer: Andrew Koningen.

Nuovi Cedrini
Happycentro
Left, bottom: Happycentro designed this poster for the band Nuovi Cedrini. 'Nuovi Cedrini' in Italian sounds like 'New Lemons', so the designers decided to recreate their logo and their silhouettes as lemon juice packs. This was a collective project in collaboration with illustrator Andrea Rania of *endriu.com* for Scalacolore – a design community based in Verona, Italy. Photos: Federico Padovani.

Mozambique
Happycentro
Above: Happycentro's poster *Mozambique*, featuring typography created from toy soldiers, was produced for the exhibition 'Imagining Mozambique', launched in 2009. The travelling art show was a fundraising drive for ASEM, a non-profit organization that helps the children of Mozambique. Designer: Federico Galvani; photos: Federico Padovani. With the support of Jamie N. Kim, Mo Manager and Wieden+Kennedy.

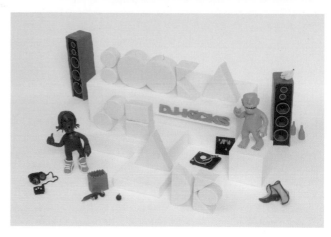

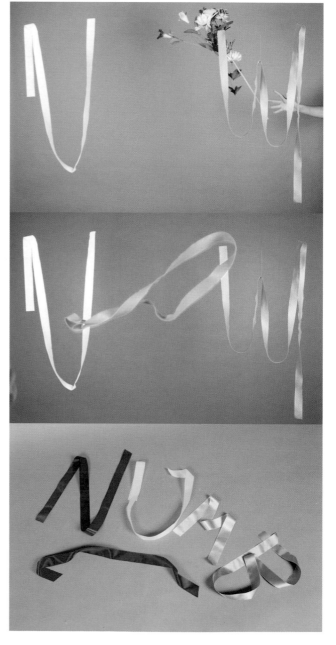

AlphaBeasts
Helen Mycroft
Left, far left: Helen Mycroft is a graphic designer from Sydney who splits her time between her two home countries of Australia and England. Her self-initiated *AlphaBeasts* are made of paper and found objects.

Booka Shade: DJ Kicks
Hort
Left, top, right: Berlin-based Hort (formerly known as Eike's Grafischer Hort) is run by Eike König. 'Hort' is a direct

translation of the studio's mission – a creative playground and a place where 'work and play' can be said in the same sentence. Shown here is Hort's first layout for the DJ Kicks album *Booka Shade*.

Vow and Numb
Helena Dietrich
Left, bottom, right: Helena Dietrich is based in Stuttgart, Germany. She works as a freelance graphic designer and on her own self-initiated networking projects, including

Vow – a shop and gallery in Stuttgart and a magazine she co-edits and art-directs with Denise Amann. Denise was also involved in creating the *Vow* ribbon shots.

Void
Huy Vu
This page, top: Huy Vu is a graphic designer based in New York City. *Void*, from 2009, was created as part of his thesis work at the Rhode Island School of Design.

Tiefschwarz
Helena Dietrich
This page, bottom: Flyer and poster for Tiefschwarz Concert, 2007. Photos: David Spaeth.

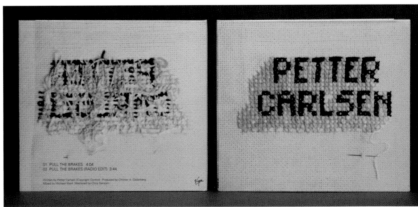

Teser om eksistensen av kjærlighet
Handverk

Left, top: Handverk is a design company based in Norway that was formed in 2009 by Eivind S. Platou and Kåre Martens. As the name 'Handverk' suggests, the studio approaches most projects with a tactile and handmade sensibility. This typographic cover for a book by author Torben Guldberg, commissioned by publisher Cappelen Damm, was designed by Handverk and photographed by Pål Laukli.

Hotel Borg
Handverk

Left, bottom: Designed by Handverk's Eivind S. Platou and photographed by Pål Laukli, this cover for Nicola Lecca's book *Hotel Borg* was also created for publishing house Cappelen Damm.

Paradox
Handverk

This page, top: Handverk were commissioned by Paradox Film to create new idents for them – short clips shown before a

feature film starts. Handverk brings the letters to the set of each new film the company produces; the letters are placed on the actual movie set and the designers film them for a few seconds. These images then become the new ident.

Petter Carlsen
Handverk

This page, bottom: Designed by Kåre Martens of Handverk, this record cover for Petter Carlsen's album released by EMI, Norway, was made using cross-stitch.

The Road to Copenhagen
Handverk
Handverk created these typographic pieces in collaboration with photo/post-production firm Gosu Design for TV2, Norway. The installations were created for an opening title as well as different idents for a major TV programme shown during the Copenhagen climate conference in 2009. Handverk decided to create all the typography by hand using recycled materials. The show was broadcast from the new opera house in Oslo, which offered an attractive setting in which to film the letters.

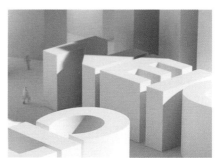

Victoria is Changing
Hat-trick

Left, top: Property developer Land Securities was planning a number of schemes to develop the area of Victoria in London. The company briefed design studio Hat-trick to utilize a poster site on Palace Street in Victoria to herald the fact that 'Victoria is changing', without going into specifics about the future developments. 2,000 recycled plastic windmills were screwed onto a printed panel, spelling out the word 'change'. These constantly spun in the strong winds and provided a talking point for local businesses and residents. Creative direction: Gareth Howat, David Kimpton and Jim Sutherland; design: Alex Swatridge.

Ebbsfleet Valley/Earthworks
Hat-trick

Left, bottom: These pictures, taken in 2009 at Land Securities' Ebbsfleet Valley site in Kent, UK, were used as key visuals in a brochure created to tell the 'story of the site so far'. The site was treated as a giant canvas to display seven earthworks, each illustrating a key point of the development.

Urbanism & Architecture
Hat-trick

Above: These visuals were created in 2009 as an identity for John Thompson & Partners (JTP) using architectural models and figures. Hat-trick asked their client to plan and build an architectural model from their own name and key words. Hat-trick then populated this with architectural figures. For use on stationery and reports, the model was shot from different angles. For use on presentations and the internet, the whole scene was filmed under different lighting conditions. For the company's new offices, the model was mounted on a wall in the main client area.

A.DePedrini   Via Vallarsa 8   Dal 1920
20139 Milano   clichés, fotolito
Telefono 02.574041161   elaborazione di immagini
Telefax 02.5520166   per la stampa

I M M A G I N I   P E R   T U T T I   I   C A R A T T E R I

100 Pieces of Havana
Intercity
Left: In 2008, London-based
graphic design studio Intercity
curated the exhibition '100
Pieces of Havana', for rum
producers Havana Club. Intercity
commissioned 100 leading
international artists and
designers to produce a piece of
artwork using Havana Club rum
and Cuban culture as their
inspiration. As well as curating
the exhibition, Intercity also
designed the project identity,
creating the '100' logo from

exactly 100 circles. As a centre-
piece to the show, the logo was
recreated as an installation, using
100 actual bottles of Havana
Club rum. To achieve the desired
effect, the bottles were set into
a purpose-built unit, which was
also illuminated from within. The
exhibition was open for 100
hours only and took place at the
Dray Walk Gallery in the Truman
Brewery, London.

De Pedrini pebble alphabet
Italo Lupi
Above: These pebbles were
picked up by the son of Milan-
based graphic designer Italo
Lupi, and his son's girlfriend,
while enjoying walks along a
beautiful beach in Tuscany. *'Sun,
sand, pebbles, blasts from the
past, cabins and bikinis was the
right cocktail'* that inspired Italo
Lupi to design this 1992 poster
for his client De Pedrini, a
Milan-based colour preparation
firm for printing. For this book,
we took the liberty of setting the

name 'Italo Lupi' using the
pebbles – they are not part of
the original poster.

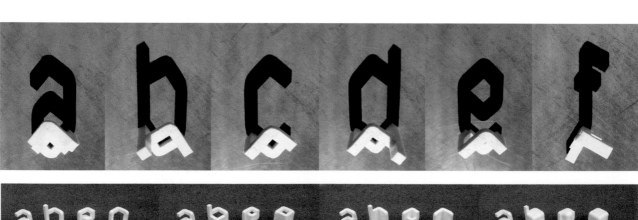

Crafts Council Collect 2009
John Morgan studio

Left, top: John Morgan studio was established in 2000 in London. Here, a signage system using silver helium balloons was an effective and elegant way to ensure no fixtures or fittings would damage the gallery interior of the international art fair for contemporary objects.

Typography and Space
(Theres) Jörger

Left, bottom: Forming one half of Jörger-Stauss (see page 116), Zürich-based graphic designer Theres Jörger created these pieces while still working solo in 2001. These spatial type designs are only a few examples of a huge body of work created for this project, examining elementary possibilities and ideas of three-dimensional typography. Numerous tangible approaches explored readability from different angles.

Voices of White City public poem
John Morgan studio

Above: Shown here is a BBC public art project in collaboration with the British poet Andrew Motion, from 2003. This poem was part of a wider programme of public lettering and landscape poetry at the BBC's White City site in London. Here was an opportunity for a piece of lettering conceived at the commencement of building as an intrinsic and integral part of the architecture and landscape. In effect it is a mosaic, where the letters and surfaces are on the same plane. The scale is such that it is as if the landscape has begun to speak for itself. The letterforms were created using variations in stone colour. The background of 90 mm (3²/₃in) square silver granite setts was contrasted with darker granite letterforms; the effect is like a binary system where zeros and ones are converted into silver and grey granite stones.

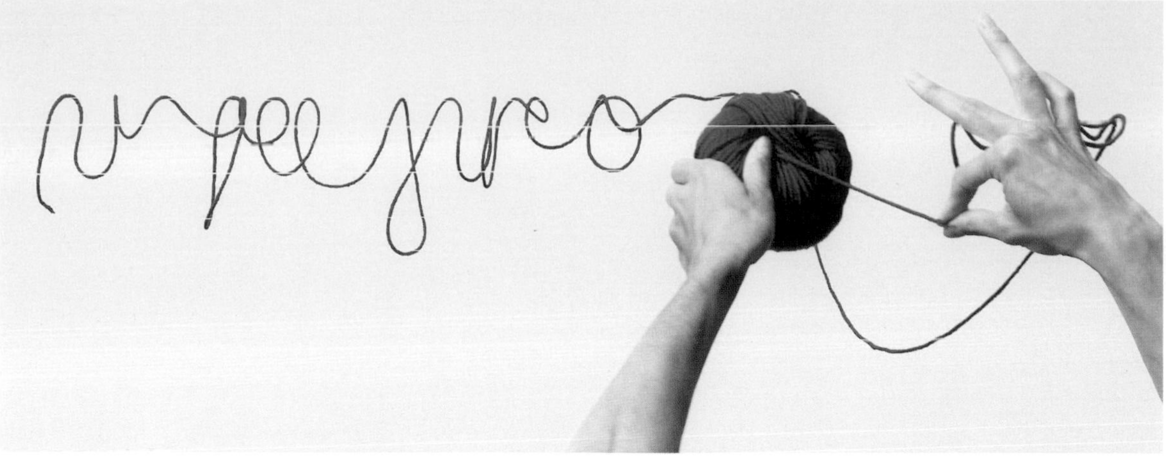

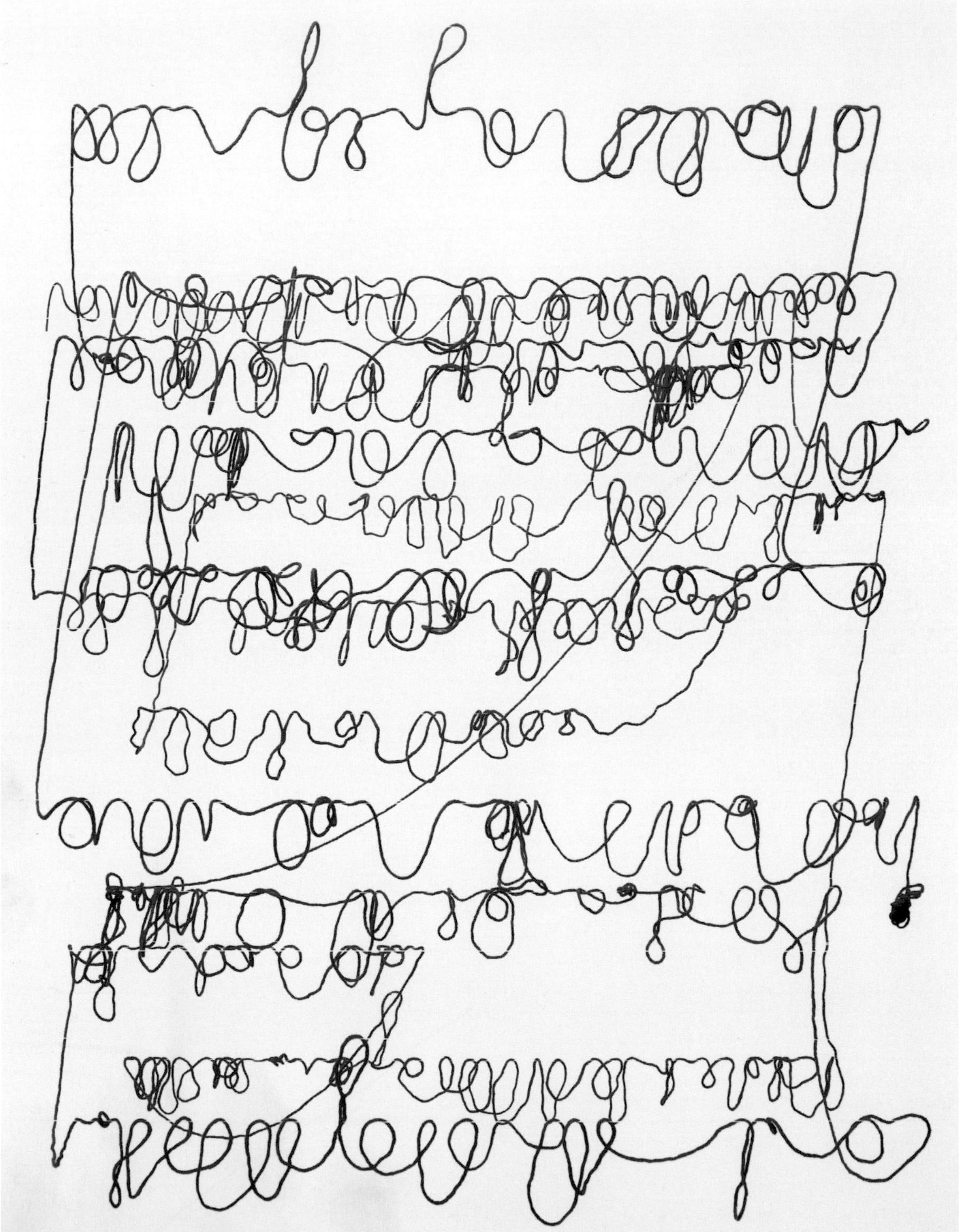

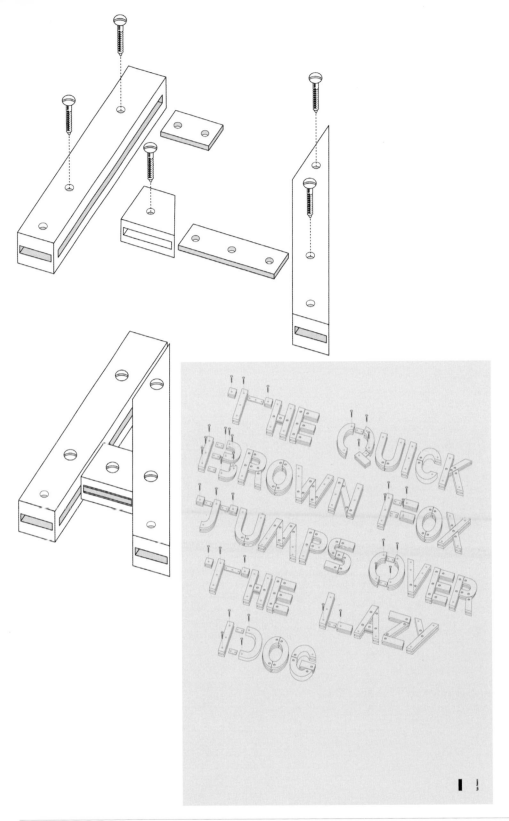

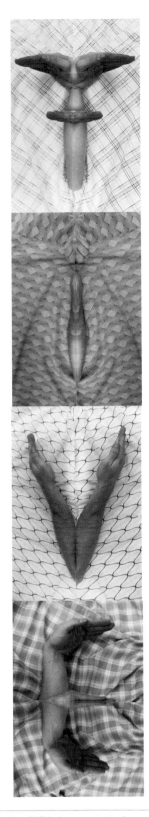

Days of Literature
Jörger-Stauss
Left: Theres Jörger and photographer Susanne Stauss have been creating typographical treatments since 2002 for the the Rhaeto-Romantic Days of Literature, an annual happening in Domat/Ems, Switzerland. This event has allowed the team to explore language and typography in space ever since. If you find it difficult to read the text of this beautiful piece, don't worry – Rhaeto-Romance languages are part of a very rare Romance

language sub-family that includes languages spoken only in north and northeastern Italy and Switzerland.

Objectography
Jamie Hearn
This page, left: Central Saint Martins graduate Jamie Hearn created the *Objectography* typeface in 2008 from a coherent set of assembly components, comprised of 30 specific components and a total of 340 separate pieces per alphabet. The letterforms

are displayed in two ways: in exploded view to illustrate how they are constructed, and the view once their pieces have been joined. The typeface is represented in the style of an information graphic and has been reproduced through the medium of posters.

Five
Jan von Holleben
This page, right: Jan is a photographer and artist who lives and plays in Berlin, Germany. For the fifth anniversary of Chinese

magazine *1626*, Jan was invited along with four other artists to create a special photo series. He picked the finest shirts from his wardrobe, a mirror, and used the shirts as backgrounds for his (free) hand. The magazine issue in question was released in March 2010.

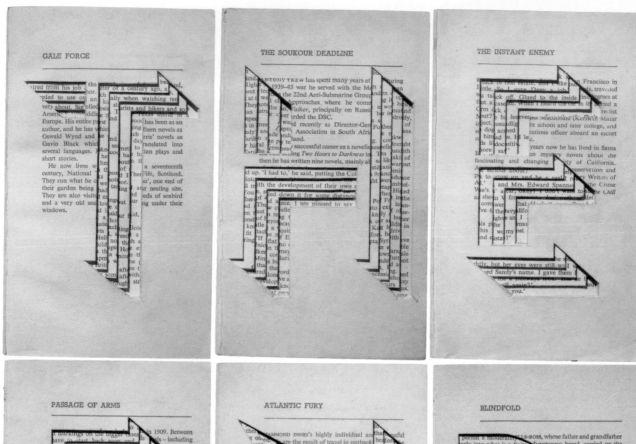

GALE FORCE

THE SOUKOUR DEADLINE

THE INSTANT ENEMY

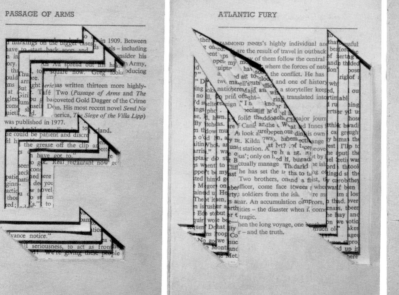

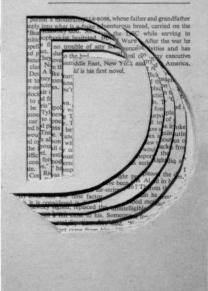

PASSAGE OF ARMS

ATLANTIC FURY

BLINDFOLD

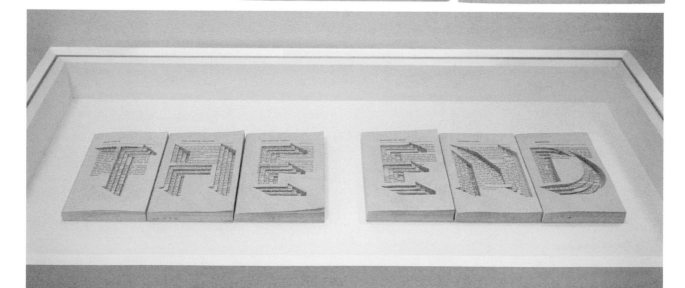

The End
Jonathan Hall
Left: Glasgow-based graphic designer Jonathan Hall took cheap and essentially discarded second-hand books, removed their purpose as literature and redefined their function. By cutting the letters out of the books, their identity remains familiar, but the viewer is encouraged to read them differently as objects. With the steady growth of the internet and the development of devices such as smart phones and e-book readers, we have been warned about the inevitable 'End of Press'. The physicality of the book may be lost in an increasingly digital age.

Paint it All
Juan Camilo Rojas
Above: Colombian-born and Miami-based graphic designer Juan Camilo Rojas created *Paint it All* for a series of postcards he designed for one of his clients, a local painting company. The project was inspired by the work of camouflage artists such as Desiree Palmen. The client was looking for a campaign that would show his company being able to service any type of paint job needed.

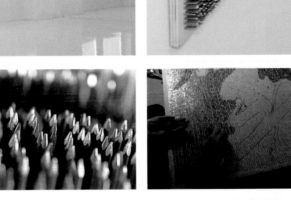

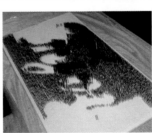

Flavor

Juan Camilo Rojas

Left, top: *Flavor* was part of an installation series created in 2008 by graphic designer Juan Camilo Rojas. His aim was to expose audiences to a particular idea through the power of typography and demonstrate how it could communicate and represent outside the usual screen- and print-based forms. This piece was created using more than 3,800 cigarettes to spell out the word 'Flavor'. The cigarettes that are half-smoked show the nicotine in the filters. *Flavor* was intended to raise awareness about the dangers of smoking cigarettes.

Gold

Juan Camilo Rojas

Left, bottom: part of the same series, *Gold* is a piece that criticizes a very popular fast food company and the obesity problem faced in our society. The piece was created by using golden-coloured French fries. The word 'gold' has different associations; it portrays the main colour of the logo of this company; it is the colour of the fries; and it portrays the associations made between the brand and society. The company's marketing campaigns depict this food as something very desirable, especially for children, thereby helping to create a society with bad eating habits and health problems such as obesity.

Enjoy

Juan Camilo Rojas

Above: This piece illustrates a word normally associated with the brand being criticized. It was created using more than 18,000 nails, which were first rusted by being immersed in the beverage produced by the brand. Juan's aim was to illustrate the health risks of drinking the sugar-laden fizzy drink.

All three pieces measure 102 x 61cm (40 x 24 in).

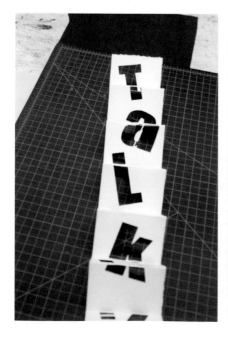

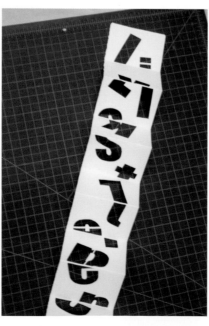

Believe/Give
Juan Camilo Rojas
Left, top: This display was created using the words 'Give', which Juan believed was appropriate for Christmas time, and the word 'Believe', which was his client's Macy's promotional word. Using more than 2,750 m (3,000 yd) of thread and steel-point pins, Juan spelled out the words to great effect.

Talk/Listen
Juan Camilo Rojas
Left, bottom: This experimental book was created to represent communication as a two-way channel.

Posi+ivo
Juan Camilo Rojas
Above: This piece was created to target mainly young people and increase awareness about the worldwide issue of sexually transmitted infections. This project formed part of a travelling exhibition, MTV Teen Age Clicks, which visited four countries. Juan created the piece using more than 2,800 condoms on a piece of canvas measuring 56 x 229 cm (22 x 90 in).

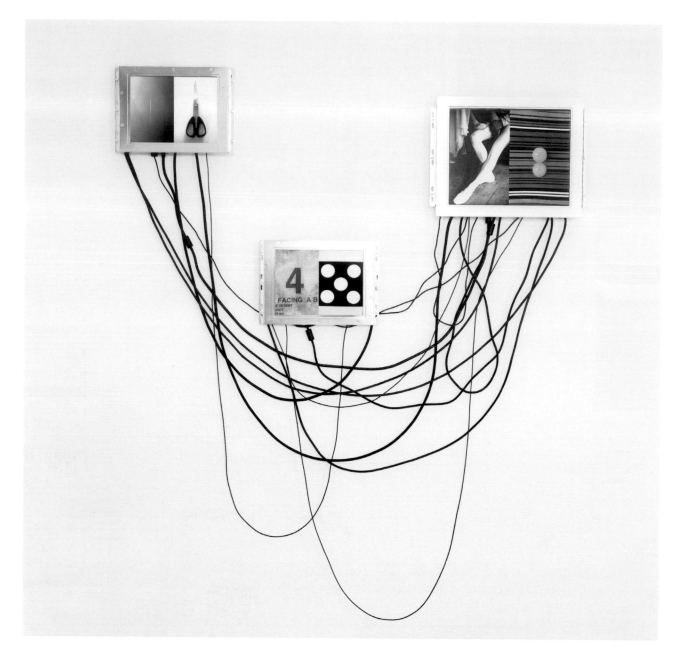

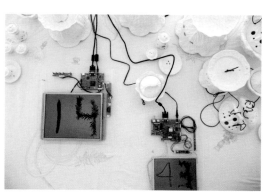

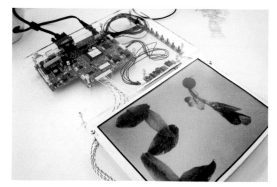

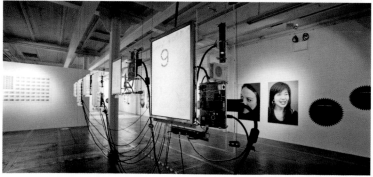

 :  :

Exquisite Clock

João Henrique Wilbert

João Henrique Wilbert is a Brazilian designer with interest and experience in interaction, design and programming. The ongoing *Exquisite Clock* project was created and developed by João at Fabrica, Italy, in 2008 with creative direction from Andy Cameron. Numbers are everywhere, if you care to see them. *Exquisite Clock* is a clock made of numbers taken from everyday life – seen, captured and uploaded by people from all over the world. Through the website *exquisiteclock.org*, users are invited to collect and upload images of numbers that can be found in different contexts around them – objects, surfaces, landscapes, cables – anything that has a resemblance to a number. The clock has an online database of numbers – an exquisite database – at its core. This supplies the website and interconnected physical platforms. *Exquisite Clock* is a multi-channel network that seeds installations, screensavers and mobile applications around the world. All numbers uploaded to the database are available to be distributed to any device connected to the internet. The application was designed so its content can be seamlessly connected and shared in real time to different platforms and devices. So far the network has seeded up to five gallery installations in Europe and the USA and recently started feeding an iPhone application – also in real time. The idea is to turn the clock into an open-ended application where its database is available in different exchange formats that any device can be connected to. *Exquisite Clock* is a relational artwork where the boundaries between artist and author, producer and consumer are blurred.

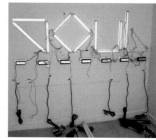
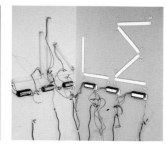

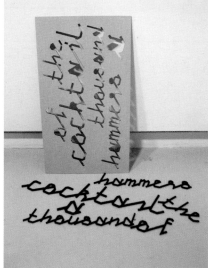

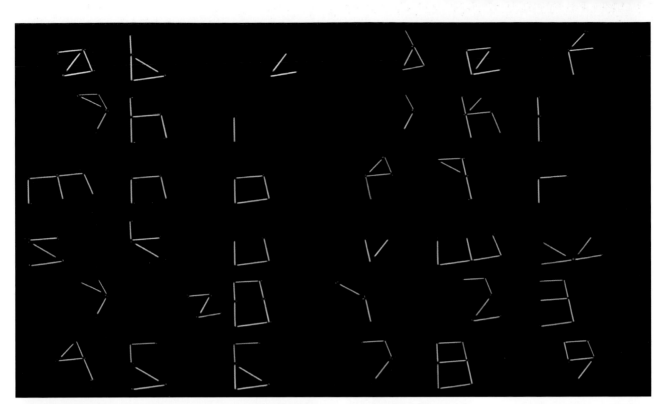

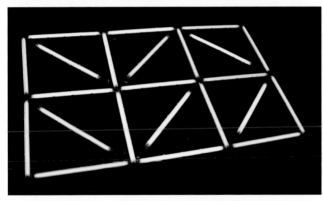

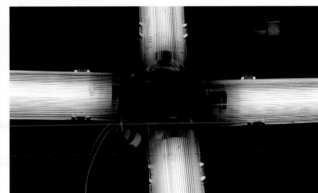

Double Death

Jan Olof Nygren

Left, top: A graduate from the School of Design and Crafts in Gothenburg, Sweden, where Jan Olof Nygren also grew up, and Cranbrook Academy of Art in Michigan, Jan splits his time and work between Europe and the USA for his freelance work. His self-initiated project *Double Death*, from 2007, used fluorescent tubes, ballasts, wire and caution tape.

The Cocktail...

Jan Olof Nygren

Left, centre: *The Cocktail of a Thousand Hammers*, a self-initiated project from 2006, is a laser-cut, spray-painted and screenprinted MDF board 3D poster.

Thug

Jan Olof Nygren

Left, bottom: Jan's self-initiated *Thug* typeface was created in 2006. It was digitally designed and then created using laser-cut plywood and spray paint. *Thug*

is a modular typeface in which the letters could be attached together for various 3D applications. It is available in two versions: STR8-UP and BLING BLING. The gold-chain look of the type inspired the name and the choice of spray paint.

NBLight

Jarrik Muller

Above: Jarrik Muller runs a design studio in Amsterdam and also works with international collaborators. One of these collaborative projects involved

Jarrik's work with Stefan Gandl at Neubau, *neubauberlin.com*. They jointly created the *NBLight* typeface shown here. First they made an analogue installation with TL lights, followed by a digital version of the typeface. The font was published in DGV's book *Neubau Modul* and is for sale through *neubauladen.com*.

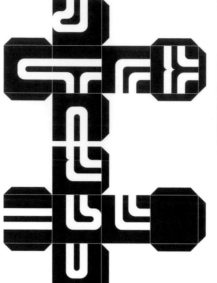

Blok
Jarrik Muller
Left, top: This typeface is made out of blocks with different shapes on each side of the cubes. The *Berlin* poster shown here was created in 2010 for the 'Show Us Your Type' project (*showusyourtype.com*). Type and layout: Jarrik Muller; illustrations: StudioBowlegs (*studiobowlegs.co.uk*).

3D Typeface
Jarrik Muller
Left, bottom: Jarrik developed this 3D typeface, which can be constructed by cutting, folding and gluing paper together.

Park Project
Jung Eun Park
This page, top: Central Saint Martins graduate Jung is a freelance illustrator now based in South Korea. The beautiful lettering for her family name was made from grass, plants and flowers.

True Stories
Jenna Burwell
This page, bottom: Graphic designer Jenna Burwell graduated from Lincoln University, UK, where she worked on an International Society of Typographic Designers (ISTD) brief called True Stories; True Geographies – putting type into the environment. Jenna chose her content to be poetry; each poem suited the environment and material it was made out of.

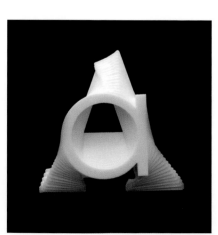

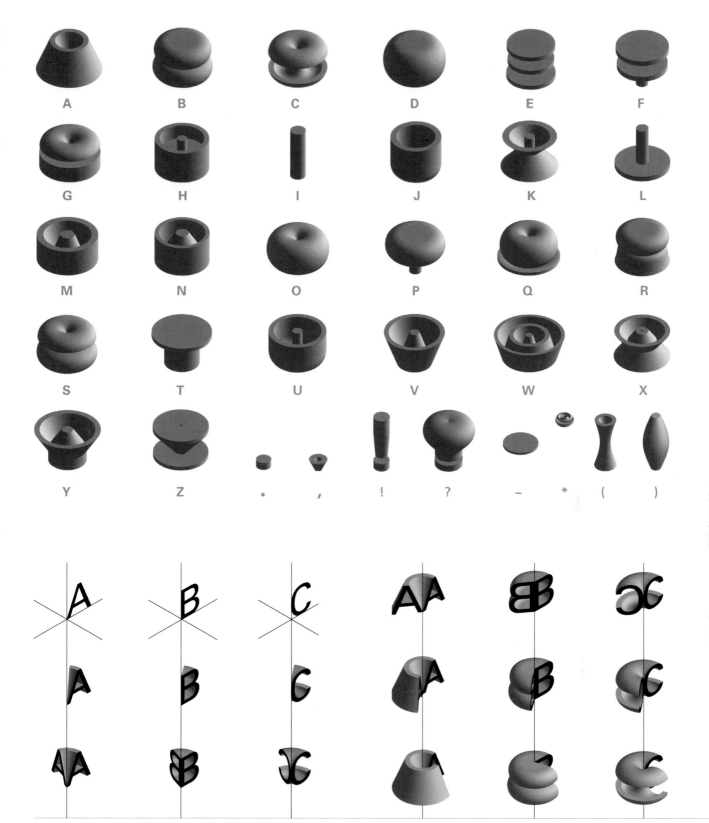

Detroit alphabet
J. Kyle Daevel
Left, top: J. Kyle Daevel is a Chicago-based designer and artist. The *Detroit* alphabet was created for 'The Shrinking Cities' exhibition, which was launched at the Museum of Contemporary Art Detroit and Cranbrook Academy of Art in 2007. The exhibition looked at industrial cities, including Detroit, that had lost populations over the last 50 years. The project included the development of this alphabet, representing the shift of a city from its pinnacle in the past to the decaying urban environment of today.

Detroit
J. Kyle Daevel
Left, bottom: Using the *Detroit* alphabet, Daevel designed a public art proposal to be placed in the Isamu Noguchi Hart Plaza in downtown Detroit. CNC stepping was employed to make a poetic relationship to Hart Plaza, which includes a concrete amphitheatre and sculptures designed by Noguchi. 'DETROIT/ Detroit' fabrication in collaboration with Brandon Davis.

Univers Revolved
Ji Lee
Above: Ji Lee is the founder of the Bubble Project and the author of two books: *Talk Back: The Bubble Project* and *Univers Revolved: a 3-Dimensional Alphabet*. To form the letters of *Univers Revolved*, a simple geometric formula was applied to the capital letters of the widely used Univers typeface: at the left-most point of each letter, a vertical axis was drawn. Then, with the help of a 3D computer program, the letters were revolved 360 degrees around the axis to form the 3D letters of the *Univers Revolved* alphabet.

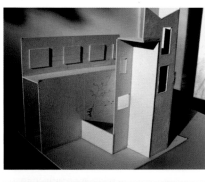

BOUQUET OF PARENTHESES FLOCK OF SOLIDUS TALK TREE

Ice

Kris Hofmann

Left, top: Originally from Austria, Kristina moved to London in 2003. A graduate from the Royal College of Art, she now works as a freelance designer and director from her East London studio. She has a particular interest in experimenting with handmade techniques and their application to animation and typographic design. *Ice* was created as part of the Oberon Book Illustration Award, a project set by the RCA CAD department and Oberon

Publishers; it won the V&A Student Illustration Award in 2009.

Bouquet of Parentheses

Kate Lyons

Left, bottom: London-based freelance graphic designer Kate Lyons graduated from Central Saint Martins in 2007. The view from the windows at the back of her house in Camden, London, was a wall and a bit of sky – typical urban living, with no access to a garden. Kate's plan was to introduce a garden to

break up the brick monotony. She worked on this site-specific lettering project, and the idea of framing a view, in her final year at Saint Martins.

Brighton Festival

Kris Hofmann

Above: The idea of this piece, created for the city of Brighton's annual arts festival, was to create a huge word-search inspired by Robert Louis Stevenson's book *Treasure Island* and have children and their parents guess the title of the book. The installation

consisted of 250 wooden letters, in the Georgia Bold typeface, in all different sizes. Both upper- and lowercase letters were assembled in a 2.5 m-high (8 ft) structure reminiscent in form and colour of the shape of a wave (appropriate for this seaside city). The size and tactile quality of the installation allowed the audience to follow the letters with both their eyes and their hands. Creative direction & design: Kris Hofmann; set building: Zain Aziz.

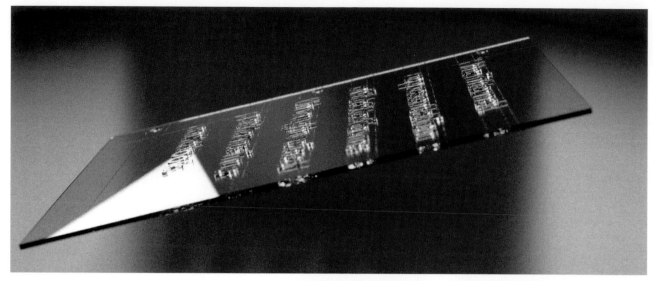

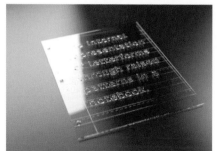

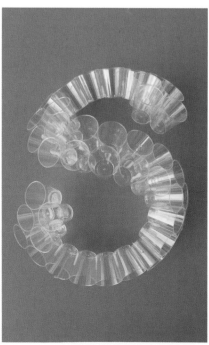

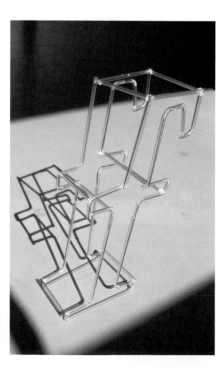

  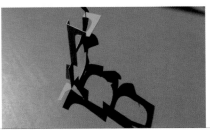

Red Meat
Karin von Ompteda

Left, top: Karin is a biologist turned graphic designer turned doctoral researcher at the Royal College of Art investigating typeface design for people with visual impairments. *'There is a moment in every designer's life when you start to see letters in everything'*, she quite rightly writes. She was a vegetarian when she conceived the project and had never touched raw meat, so the design process was punctuated with uncontrollable

gagging. Photographing the letters on a clean cutting board transformed the carnage into an aesthetically pleasing, almost sterile design project.

Cortext
Karin von Ompteda

Left, centre: Using fingertips to read involves the transformation of tactile stimuli into an internal representation. Thus it seems that people engaging in this practice are forever designing ephemeral letterforms within a sort of mental notebook. *Cortext*

was designed so that people who don't usually read embossed letters can experience the mechanical–neural transfer of text from skin to cortex. A three-dimensional replica of typical notebook paper was created through stereo-lithographic rapid prototyping. Additionally, a custom legible typeface was designed for the project. Finally, as the project was inspired by people with visual impairments, its design meets accessibility guidelines for tactile signage.

Three-dimensional typography
Karina Petersen

Left page, bottom, and above: Graphic designer Karina Petersen holds an MA in graphic design and is a 2009 graduate from Kolding School of Design, Denmark. In 2009 a book on her type experiments was published (*Three-Dimensional Typography*, see *designskolenkolding.dk*) featuring – among other pieces – the work shown here.

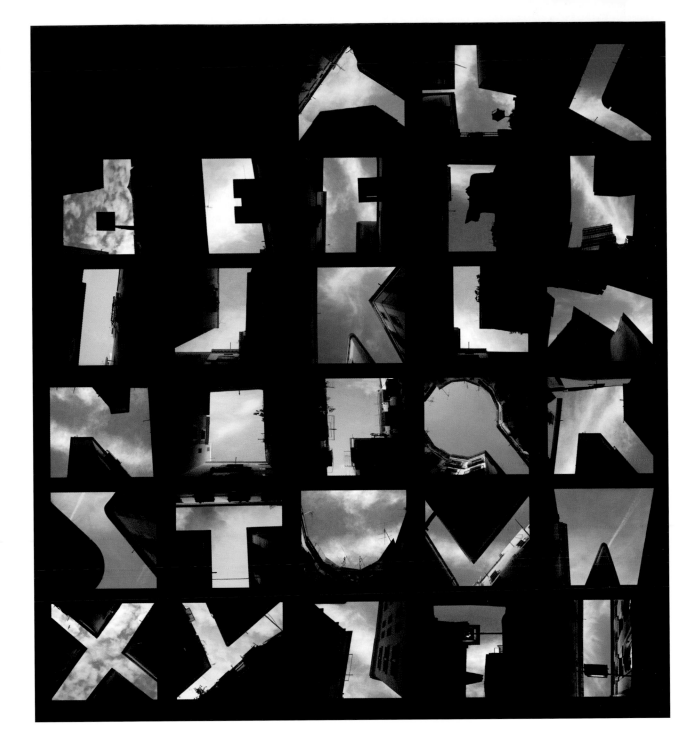

PVC Pipe
Lee Stokes
Left, top: London-based Lee Stokes works freelance under his moniker StokeS. He enjoys frequent trips to DIY stores, where he likes to collect and experiment with unusual materials that stimulate and form his design method. The *PVC Pipe* typeface was created with Britain's flooding victims in mind.

Wood is Good
Lee Basford
Left, bottom: Lee Basford is art director at Fluid in Birmingham, UK. This original T-shirt design was created for Uniqlo. In 2007, Lee was invited by Uniqlo to their Creative Awards in Japan, where he received a Judges' Choice Award for this work.

Type the Sky
Lisa Rienermann
Above: Originally from Cologne, freelance designer and photographer Lisa Rienermann now lives and works in Berlin. Her much-talked-about photographic alphabet project, *Type the Sky*, was created in 2005 when she spent a semester in Barcelona. Standing in a little courtyard, she looked up and saw houses, the sky, clouds and a letter 'Q'. The negative space in between the houses formed a letter. She loved the idea of the sky as words, the negative being the positive, and embraced the challenge of finding additional letters. In the following weeks, she kept running around looking up to the sky, and bit by bit she found all the letters of this amazing alphabet.

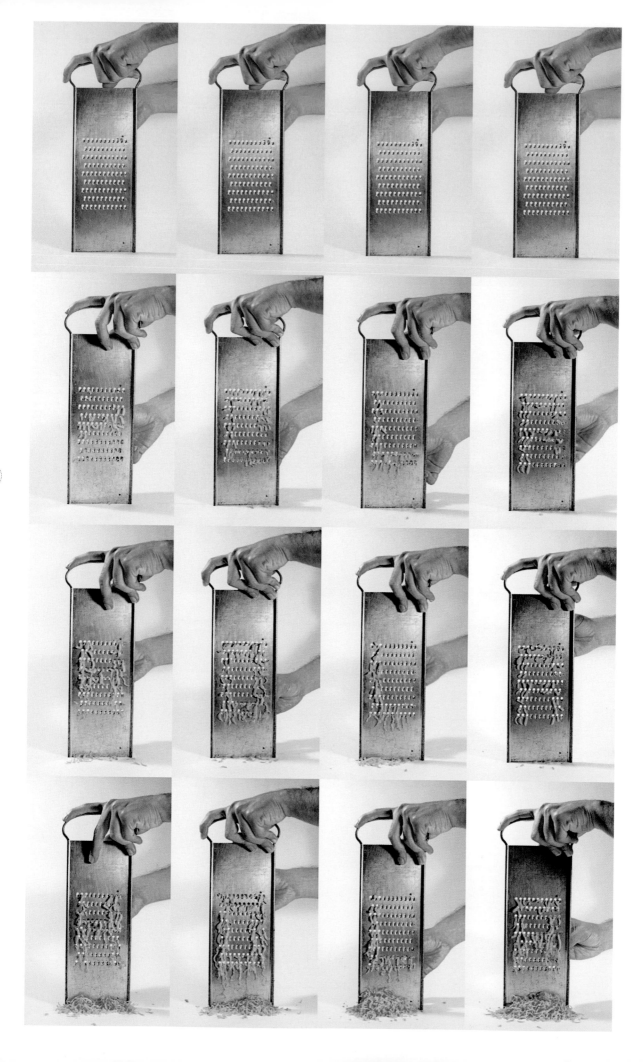

Morph

Miguel Ramirez

Left: Designer Miguel Ramirez, based in Los Angeles, grated this typographic piece using cheese to form the letters 'Hola' ('Hello'). Miguel has found that creating three-dimensional objects allows him to expand the way he approaches and solves visual problems, and leads him to a greater appreciation for embracing error.

Studio Alphabet/
Kurlansky's Krazy Kaps

Mervyn Kurlansky

Above: This work was conceived by Pentagram co-founder Mervyn Kurlansky while he was an external assessor at Preston Polytechnic, as a charitable contribution to Preston's student publication on typography. The self-imposed design constraint was to restrict the choice of found objects forming an alphabet to objects found in the Pentagram studio. The items were then individually

photographed by Pentagram's in-house photographer, and prints were made to a common height and pasted in position. The student publication was to be printed in one colour only – black – hence the black and white version. The work was produced in 1977. Some ten years later (no precise date is available), it was decided to recreate the alphabet in colour for a full-colour publication. Fortunately all the objects were still to be found in the studio. The original title was *Studio*

Alphabet. When Herb Lubalin later reproduced the alphabet in *U&lc*, he called it *Kurlansky's Krazy Kaps.*

Standard Time

Mark Formanek

Standard Time was the idea of the German artist Mark Formanek, and was realized by the Berlin-based media agency Datenstrudel. It was shown at the Media Art Festivals Transmediale (Berlin), Ars Electronica (Linz/Austria), and Tokyo Media Arts. *Standard Time* pursues a new concept in displaying time. The course of time is shown in a movie of exactly 24 hours, which shows workers constructing the time in the form of a digital display by using man-sized wooden slats – of course in real time. Like any conventional digital clock, *Standard Time* displays time using four ciphers. The first two show the hours, the second two the minutes. For the workers, this implies the following: on the stroke of 10:59 they have exactly one minute to rebuild the 0 to 1, the 5 to 0 and the 9 also to 0. Now *Standard Time* is on the 11 o'clock position. Again, there is one minute left to rebuild the last 0 to 1. And so on.... 1,611 reconstructions in 24 hours; 72 workers in four shifts, all done on a summer's day in a gap between buildings in central Berlin. *Standard Time* offers us a new perspective on the watch, because it provides more than just information about time. The eyes of the viewer automatically become caught by what is happening on the screen, because there is more to see than just the hands of a watch. It is the human ambition to keep up with the time – well known to be a difficult undertaking. During large reconstructions, for example on the hour, the workers finish in the nick of time. The spectator becomes engrossed, and forgets about the time while watching the clock.

M

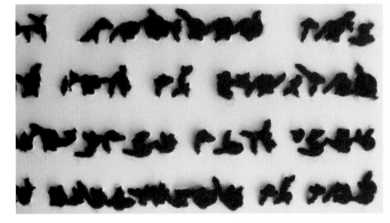

Love Type
Miguel Ramirez
Left: Miguel Ramirez collaborated with fellow designer Melissa Madrid to create a dot matrix typeface entitled *Love Type* using tennis balls placed in netting.

Beeep Beep Beeeeep
Miguel Ramirez
This page, top: Checking out at the grocery store. This three-dimensional type exploration uses foldable grocery store paper bags. *Beeep Beep Beeeeep* is one of the first 3D typefaces that

Miguel created following an encouraging experimental typography class at California State University, Long Beach, taught by Andrew Byrom (whose work also features in this book).

Dyslexic alphabet
Miranda van Hooft
This page, bottom: Dutch graphic designer Miranda van Hooft created this graduation project by hand-stitching texts into paper and then focusing on the backs of the words. Dyslexics see the shapes of letters differently

and perceive texts as a series of abstract symbols. Dyslexics also tend to be better with three-dimensional shapes than non-dyslexic people, and they often see (and write) text inverted. The project aims to raise awareness of this common condition.

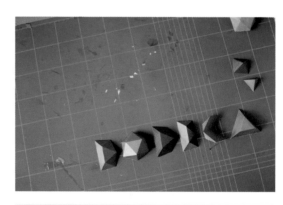

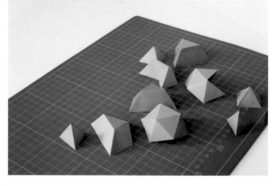

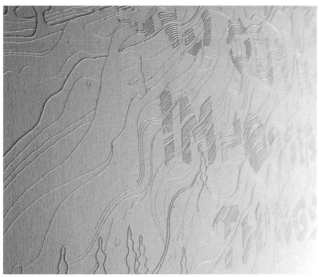

Embroidered envelope
Michelle Jones
Left, top: Michelle Jones enjoys working with hand-drawn and physical 3D type. Her business cards, for instance, feature reproduced contact details that were hand-sewn into felt. She also sends out unique CVs created using a sewing machine. This technique helps to give her work a more personal feel and has more impact. Shown here is the beautiful envelope in which she sent us her submission for this book.

Dodeca
Michael Hübner
Left, bottom: The experimental typeface *Dodeca*, by Basel-based, German graphic designer Michael Hübner, is based on the diverse spacial constructions that can be built from equilateral triangles. *Dodeca* was not conceived at the computer, but developed using paper, scissors and glue. The results are playful characters that resemble crystals that could be combined to build bigger structures.

Twilight embroidery
Mario Hugo
Above: This self-initiated typographic panel, full title *Twilight, Gravity, and Our Many Impossible Things*, was designed in 2009 by New York-based artist and designer Mario Hugo as a signed limited edition. It is hand-embroidered with silk and cotton threads on hemp/silk fabric and hand-stretched over a 7.6 cm (3 in) wooden frame. The piece was inspired by watching his girlfriend and business partner Jennifer, who has a

background in fashion, work with fabric and textiles. Mario wanted to see his two-dimensional typographic piece extruded into a three-dimensional relief, and the piece was sent away to India to be hand-embroidered. The whole piece measures 106.7 x 139.7 cm (42 x 55 in).

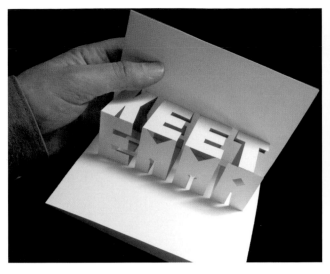

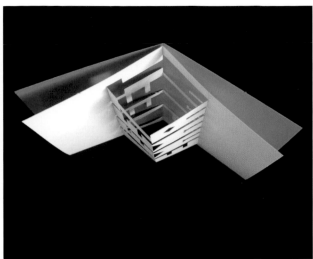

No Rules
Me Studio
Left: Me Studio is a small graphic design studio founded in 2005 in Amsterdam by British designer Martin Pyper. The studio has created numerous 3D type projects, including the experimental typeface *No Rules* – a work in progress, as they point out. It was a collaboration between studio founder Martin Pyper and Uwe Steffen. They embraced the restrictions of the ruler's sections with folding joints and the way the two-meter-long ruler can be shaped to make the necessary letterforms for a coherent typeface.

Keet Card
Me Studio
This page, top: A three-dimensional card to announce the birth of baby 'Keet' (Kate). Printed on stiff white card in two Pantone colours, then laser-cut to create pop-up letters and dotted fold-lines, the card pops open by itself when taken out of the envelope.

Monodot
Me Studio
This page, bottom: Monodot is an independent film production company operating out of Brussels, Belgium, since 2009. Me Studio was commissioned to develop their corporate identity. The starting point for this playful and ever-evolving identity was the company name, which suggests 'one dot', whereas the word itself contains three dots (or rather letter o's). All the letter o's are replaced with found (round) objects and

ephemera collected by the three Monodot founders. The resulting shoebox full of weird and personal objects became the basic ingredients for a set of varied and reguarly renewed logos. Photos: Femke Hulshof.

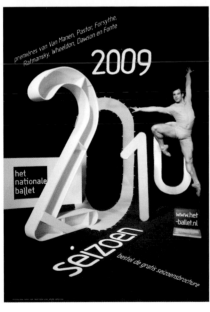

We Jane
Me Studio
Left, top: Small communication agency We Jane specializes in 'female marketing'. Their identity, developed by Me Studio, was made using ribbons to create a subtly feminine look and feel. Each person in the company has their own unique logo in a different-coloured ribbon. Photos: Femke Hulshof.

Yesterday
Me Studio
Left, bottom: This typographic installation by collaborators Martin Pyper and former intern Dylan Polak was made from the 3,000 recycled jewel cases Martin was left with after ripping his CD collection to iTunes. The team built the line *'Yesterday, all my troubles seemed so far away'*, a quote from the Beatles song, as a comment on the plastic waste created by these defunct boxes. *Yesterday* was built in 2009 at the Royal Art Academy

in The Hague, the Netherlands, and has since been exhibited several times at art events.

Dutch National Ballet posters
Me Studio
Above: These posters, advertising the 2009/10 season for long-term client the Dutch National Ballet, feature pure photographs of stage sets featuring all the relevant information without any digital intervention. Apart from the posing dancers and props, the image also features a number of *trompe l'oeil* effects,

such as the number zero that is cut into two parts in front and behind the dancer. The four numbers that form '2010' are all very different sized elements that were placed in the set to appear to be the same size. Designer: Martin Pyper; photos: Ruud Baan; set design: Me Studio/Gloudy & Sons.

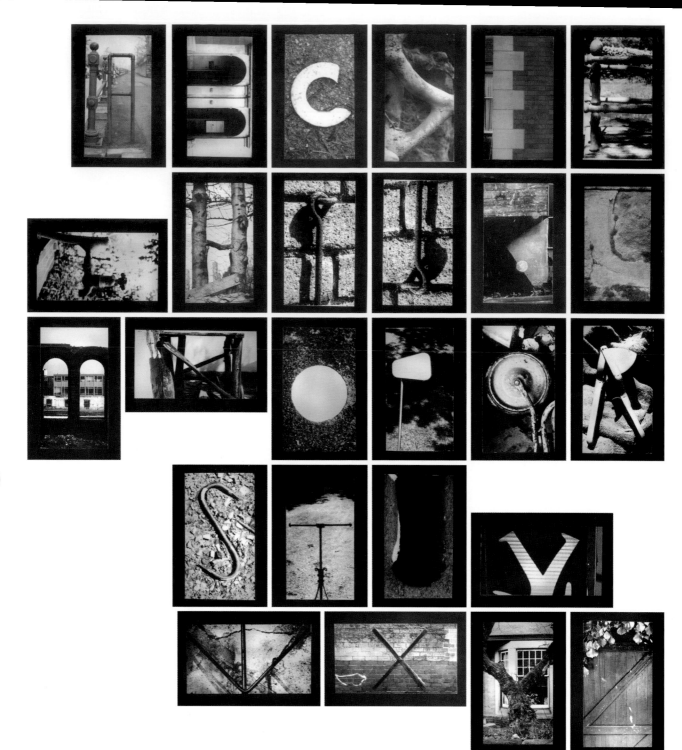

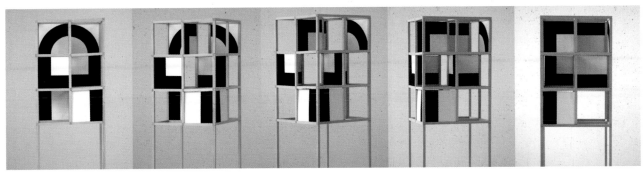

1976 Alphabet
Mesh Design

Left: Mesh Design was formed in 2008 by four graduates based in the Midlands, UK. This alphabet was created by Tony Ellis, the father of Mesh Design's director Sam Ellis. All photographs were taken on a walk through Derby in 1976. Sam follows in the footsteps of his father, and his grandfather, who were both graphic designers, specializing in typography.

Polygraph system
Merci Bernard

Above: French graphic designer Thomas Bernard founded Merci Bernard in 2007. He is also a member of the French graphic collective Think Experimental. His *Polygraph* system makes it possible to transform any letter into another when walking around it. This system is composed of two elements, a wooden structure and square modules of varnished paperboards, each painted with a black line, curve or angle. Each letter is made up of

six parts. The various modules on offer (square, full, curved, etc) make it possible to create many different letters. The four sides of the structure can show four different letters or signs, which passers-by can read only when they are in the right position.

 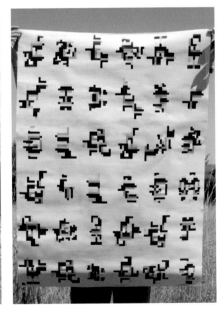

Anamorphosis
Merci Bernard
Left: Similar to his work on the *Polygraph* system (see previous page), these anamorphic experiments also explore shape-shifting letterforms. These letters either transform from one letter into another as the vantage point changes, or the sculpted letter stays the same – an equally fascinating effect.

Gyroide
Merci Bernard
Above: *Gyroide* is an anamorphic font that can be read perfectly at a 90-degree angle while the viewer moves around it. Astonishingly, each letter was made from only one piece of paper that was cut, folded and glued together to create the sculptural letters.

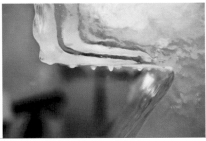

Festival du Mot
Merci Bernard

Left: All the elements of this theatrical ad were handmade with paper. Created for the 2006 Festival du Mot, based in La Charité Sur Loire, France, all words in this composition are three-dimensional and take centre-stage.

Ozon
MAGMA Brand Design

Above: Guerilla Utopia was a series of events conceived by German agency MAGMA Brand Design, who usually focus on corporate and brand design. These thought-provoking interpretations of aspirations, fears and visions of today's society were launched with *Ozon* in July 2004. Four letters were carved out of ice, each letter weighing a tonne. The work was prominently placed in the city centre of the agency's native

Karlsruhe. *Ozon* was installed early in the morning and by the end of that fine summer day the letters had melted away. All that was left were the details of a website that featured project information and further links. Photos: Jochen Sand/Sandwerk.

 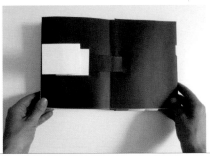 

ABC 3D

Marion Bataille

Paris-based Marion Bataille is a freelance graphic designer specializing in book covers, typography and illustration. She graduated from ESAG Penninghen in 1988 and published her first book in 1999. Her alphabet pop-up book *ABC 3D* made a big splash internationally when it was released around the globe in 2008 by publishers including Bloomsbury, Carlsen and Albin Michel. Letters not only pop up, but some also move and transform. Shown with kind permission of Marion Bataille and Editions Albin Michel, Paris.

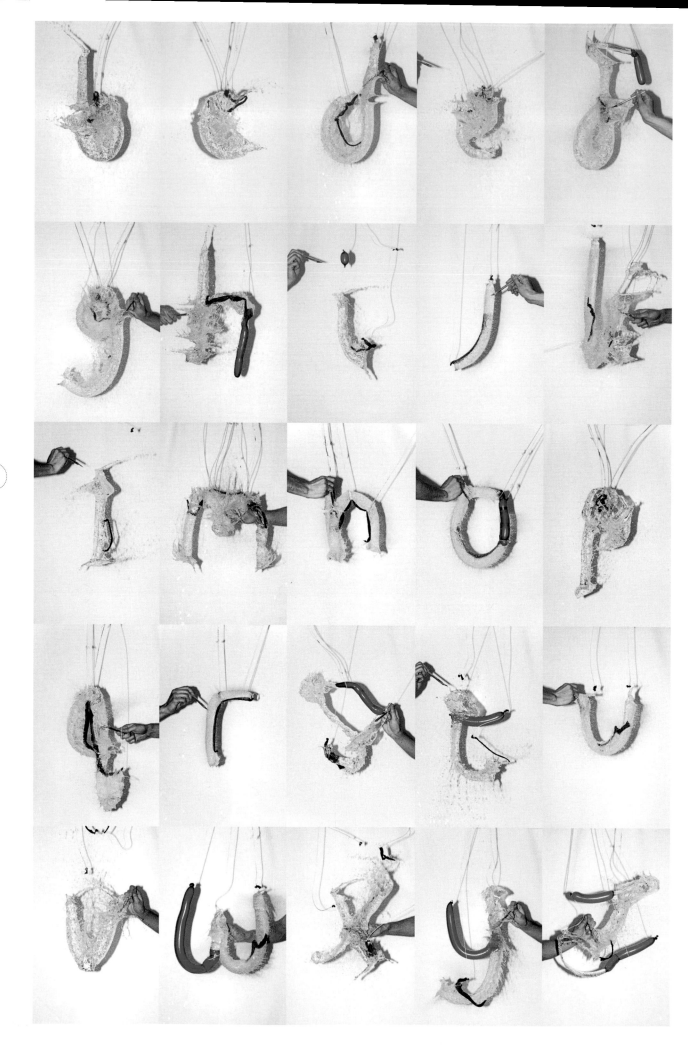

Waterform

MoreGood

MoreGood founders Ralph Hawkins and Amy Ricketts from Surrey, UK, are fascinated by aspects of coincidence. They created the *Waterform* typeface when trying to find a method of producing self-generated letterforms. Following many experiments, they decided to work with balloons filled with water. Timing was key to capturing each balloon bursting, leaving behind a trace of the letter for just a split second.

These specific moments created a unique letterform every time, representing the fleeting nature of spoken language.

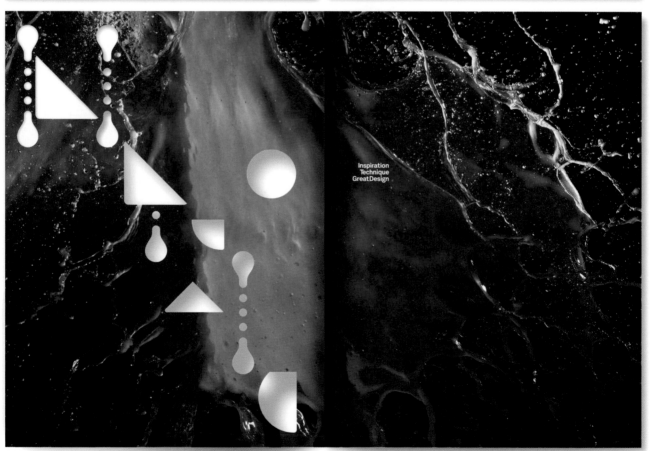

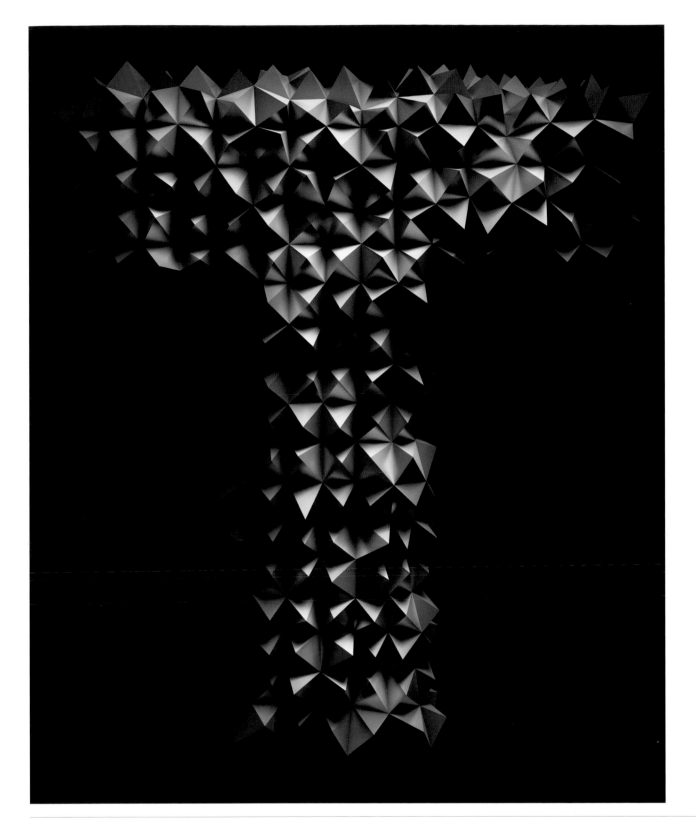

Computer Arts 163
Non-Format
Left: The creative direction and
design team Kjell Ekhorn
(Norwegian) and Jon Forss
(British) of Non-Format are
based in Oslo and Minneapolis
respectively. In 2009, they were
commissioned by *Computer Arts*
magazine (Future Publishing) to
create this cover and opening
spread. The cover is die-cut and
scored so that, once folded out,
the shapes spell out the word
'BIRTH'. Inside spread photo:
Non-Format and Jake Walters.

Tijana T
Nemanja Jehlicka
Above: Belgrade-based Nemanja
Jehlicka was commissioned by
ad agency McCann Erickson to
create visuals, including the B0-
sized poster shown here, for a
book entitled *Fresh*. The poster
was folded and inserted into the
book. *Fresh* started as a blog
featuring local talent such as
musicians, illustrators and actors.
The brief for Nemanja's poster
was to illustrate the 'T' of Tijana,
a DJ, producer and TV host.

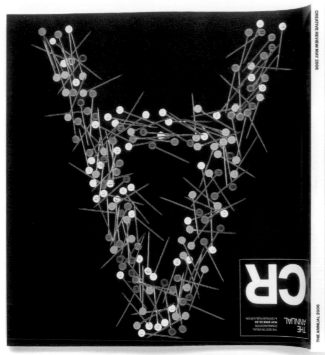

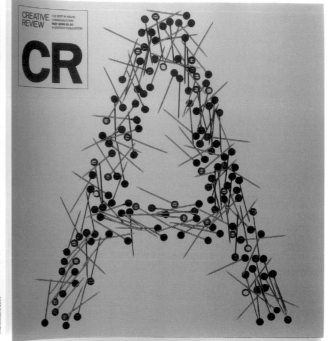

CREATIVE REVIEW THE BEST IN VISUAL COMMUNICATION MAY 2006 £5.50 A CENTAUR PUBLICATION

CR

THE ANNUAL
SPECIAL ISSUE

INCLUDES OVER 100 EXTRA PAGES OF THE BEST WORK OF THE YEAR IN VISUAL COMMUNICATION

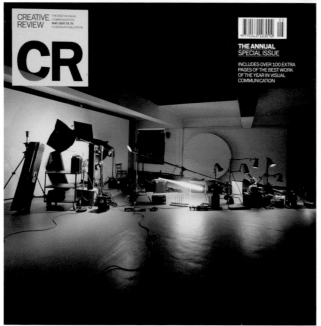

THE ANNUAL THE BEST IN VISUAL COMMUNICATION MAY 2007 £3.70 A CENTAUR PUBLICATION

CR

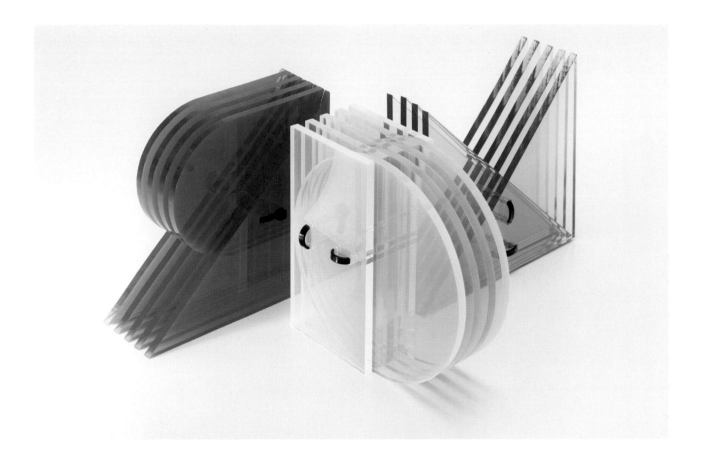

The Annual cover, 2006
Nathan Gale
Left, top: This cover features a recreation of *Creative Review*'s *The Annual* 'A' logo using map pins. Former *Creative Review* art director Nathan Gale commissioned Design Project to design the front and back cover. It was printed using MetalFX – a silver-based ink that produces more than 600 different metallics when used in conjunction with standard CMYK. *Creative Review* editor: Patrick Burgoyne.

The Annual cover, 2007
Nathan Gale
Left, bottom: Another recreation of the 'A' logo commissioned by former *Creative Review* art director Nathan Gale – this time using equipment from a photography studio – for the front cover of *Creative Review*'s awards issue *The Annual, 2007*. The smaller-scale images were created prior to the main cover image as part of a campaign to advertise *The Annual*. Front and back cover photos: Dan Tobin Smith, *dantobinsmith.com*, with

assistance by Kate Jackling and Tom Brown; retouching: Martin Pryor at Bayeux; *Creative Review* editor: Patrick Burgoyne.
(See also *The Annual cover, 2010* on page 53.)

Illustrated Children's Books Denmark
NR2154
Above: Established by Jacob Wildschiødtz and Troels Faber, NR2154 is a multi-disciplinary design studio based in Copenhagen and New York. Commissioned by the Danish

Arts Council's Literature Centre, these letters are made of laser-cut 5 mm (⅕ in) acrylic glass in fluorescent colours. The pieces (12 cm/4¾ in high) are tied together with strips. Designed by Troels Faber with assistance by Ulrik Ejlers; photos: Timme Hovind.

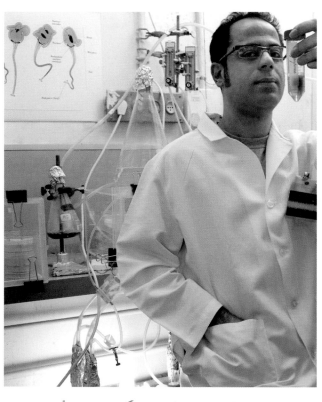

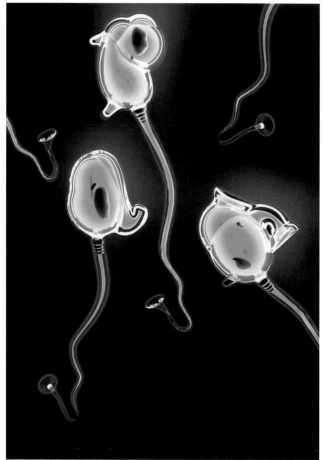

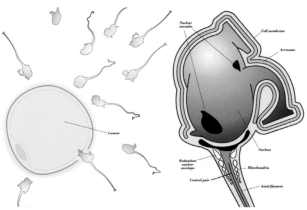

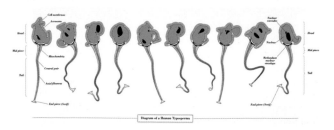

Diagram of a Human Typosperma

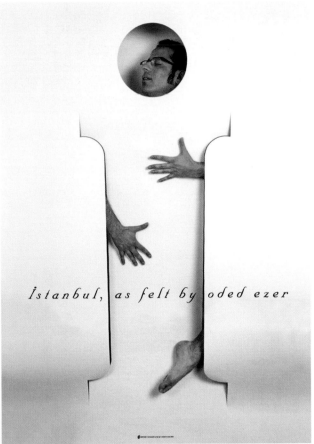

Istanbul, as felt by oded ezer

Typo-ants
Oded Ezer

Left, top: Graphic designer Oded Ezer runs his own studio, Oded Ezer Typography, from Givatayim, Israel. *Typo-ants*, from 2005/06, was art directed and designed by Oded and photographed by Idan Gil. They are from Oded's first 'biotypography' project – the name Oded gave to his idea of biology-based typography. He explains that biotypography is any typographical application that uses biological systems, living organisms or derivatives thereof, to create or modify typographical phenomena.

Typosperma
Oded Ezer

Left, bottom: *Typosperma*, from 2006, is part of Oded's second biotypography project. It features cloned sperm that have typographic information implanted into their DNA, and also diagrams of human 'typo-sperma'. The picture showing Oded as a typo-scientist was taken by Ruthie Ezer.

I (heart) Milton
Oded Ezer

This page, top, left: *I (heart) Milton*, from 2008, is a typographic homage to Milton Glaser's 'I Love NY' logo. Photo: Idan Gil.

I (heart) Istanbul
Oded Ezer

This page, top, right: This visual was designed in 2007 for a poster exhibition in Istanbul, Turkey. Photo: Idan Gil.

Open
Oded Ezer

This page, bottom: Visual from 2008 for a poster design for a company called Open Ltd.

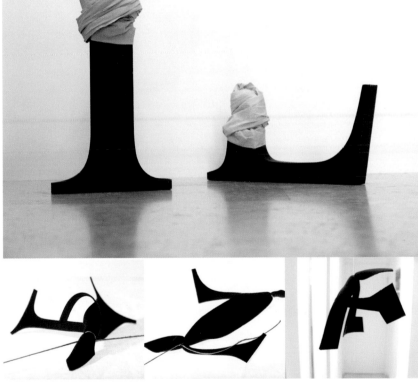

Unimportant & Nothing
Oded Ezer
Left, top: The *Unimportant & Nothing* poster from 2004 is a typographic homage to the Israeli poet Yona Volach. Photo: Shaxaf Haber.

3D Study 27 (M), 28 (E), 25 (A)
Oded Ezer
Left, bottom: Here, the letter edges are lifted from the page to create dynamic movement in space. Oded developed this technique in 2007 and later used it for several projects, including *I (heart) Milton* (see previous page).

3D Study 23 (wheel/g)
Oded Ezer
This page, top, left: Detail from the *Tybrid* series – an homage from 2007 to Marcel Duchamp's *Bicycle Wheel*.

Temporary
Oded Ezer
This page, top, centre: Details from the *Temporary Type* series, 2006.

Tortured Letters
Oded Ezer
This page, bottom: Some examples from 2006's *Tortured Letters* series. Photos: Oded Ezer and Idan Gil.

ABCollected
Open Studio
This page, right: *ABCollected* is an ongoing project by Düsseldorf-based Kai Hoffmann, co-founder of Open Studio. It took him more than three years to complete this alphabet, as none of the letterforms were arranged or digitally edited. Every single picture was the result of being in the right place at the right time and with a camera to hand.

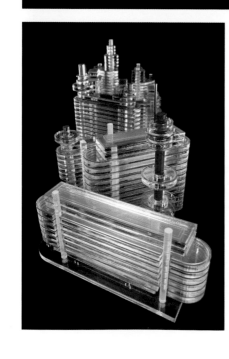

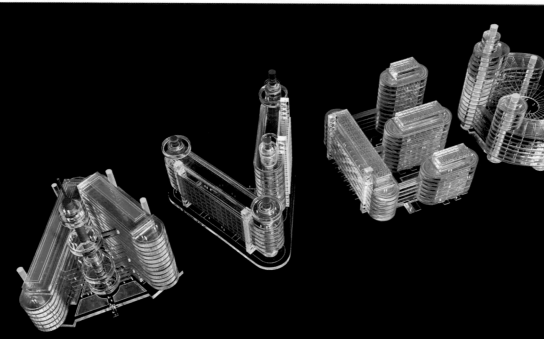

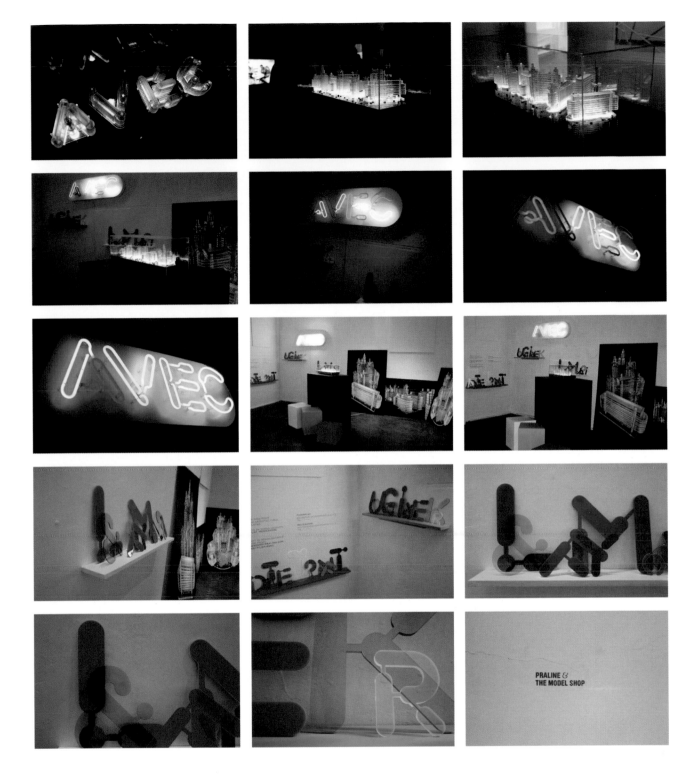

AVEC

Praline and RSHP Model Shop

In 2010, London-based design studio Praline took part in a group exhibition called 'If You Could Collaborate' (see also pages 54–55). The aim of the project was to provide a platform for creatives from all over the world to question their conventional working methods and outcomes. Praline immediately thought of the RSHP Model Shop as the ideal partner for a project based on unusual collaborations. Praline and the RSHP Model Shop had met while working together on a Richard Rogers + Architects exhibition at the Centre Pompidou in 2007. The *AVEC* project evolved from architectural floor plates to font, from font to model, from model to 3D letters, to photographs, to text and a neon sign. An actual font called *AVEC* was created and exists in three weights: Floorplay, Mezzanine and Façade. The whole process has been recorded, which brings in the fourth dimension of time. All these elements were installed as an exhibition at the A Foundation in London in January 2010. The *AVEC* font is available as a free download. Concept & creation: Praline and RSHP model shop; typography: Praline; models, including photographs used on boards in the exhibition: Mike Fairbrass at RSHP model shop; neon sign design & production: Neon Circus.

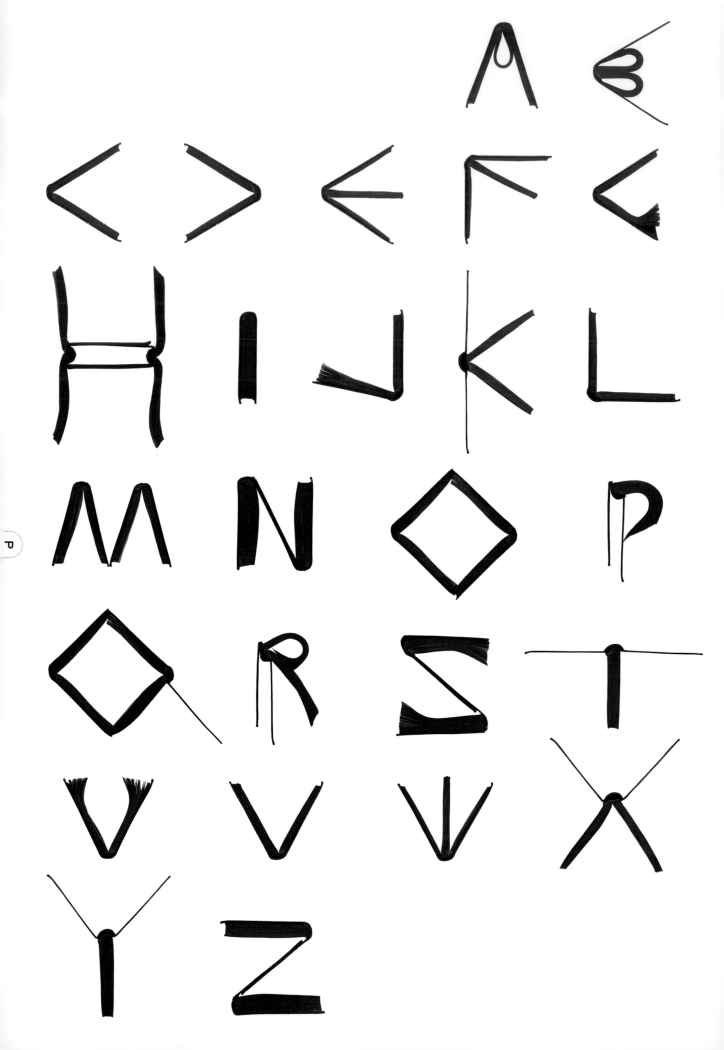

Alphabook
Pesca Salada

Left: Barcelona-based Pol Viladoms Claverol and Maria Beltran Marín work as graphic designers and photographers under the moniker Pesca Salada. For their *Alphabook* project, they reversed the relationship between books and letters and turned books (usually the 'container') into letters (the 'content'). To reinforce this idea, they looked for a special book – they wanted an old book with a hard cover, slightly damaged by time. They eventually found the ideal book, with red edges and bible paper, at a second-hand market.

Home
Post Typography

This page, top: Baltimore-based graphic design studio Post Typography created this lettering treatment for an art exhibition; it was used on postcards, posters and promotional materials. They rearranged a wall of bookshelves so that their contents spelled out the word 'HOME', the name of the exhibition. Commissioned by the creator and gallery owner Nancy Froehlich, the visual was created in 2006. Client: Gallery 2219.

John Hopkins Film Festival
Post Typography

This page, bottom, left: The Johns Hopkins Film Festival is an annual underground film festival in Baltimore. For the 2001 festival poster, Post Typography focused on the underground aspect of the festival; how it presents the leftovers and detritus of mainstream cinema. The festival title was created on a movie theatre floor, spelled out of spilt popcorn.

Metropolis magazine
Post Typography

This page, bottom, right: For the cover of *Metropolis*'s January 2010 issue, Post Typography turned the letters of the title 'What's Next' into cut-paper doors that become advent calendar-style windows into the issue's contents.

JULY 15 – 31
ARTSCAPE

AN EXHIBITION OF HAND-DRAWN LETTERING
AND EXPERIMENTAL TYPOGRAPHY
CURATED BY POST TYPOGRAPHY

Alphabet

AN EXHIBITION OF HAND-DRAWN LETTERING
& EXPERIMENTAL TYPOGRAPHY

March 11 – 31, 2006
Workhorse Gallery
4210 Santa Monica Blvd
Los Angeles, CA 90029
323-666-6163

Opening Reception:
Saturday, March 11
7:00 – 11:00 PM

ORGANIZED BY POST TYPOGRAPHY AND ARTSCAPE / PRESENTED BY WORKHORSE GALLERY / WWW.POSTTYPOGRAPHY.COM / WWW.ARTSCAPE.ORG

Alphabet: installation views
Post Typography
Left, top: Commissioned by Artscape and curated by Post Typography, each alphabet in the show 'Alphabet: An Exhibition of Hand-Drawn Lettering & Experimental Typography' was printed in black and white and displayed in identical black frames. This minimal approach was both economical and a way to visually unite a broad range of alphabets and approaches. The alphabets and typefaces – often three-dimensional – represented

the work of artists in North America, Europe and Asia, encompassing well-known typographers and designers as well as rising artists and design students. Following the launch in Baltimore, the 'Alphabet' show travelled around the USA from 2005 through 2009. The poster and catalogue of this influential exhibition are also shown here.

May
Post Typography
This page, top: This typographic illustration opened the May

2008 calendar section of *Fast Company* magazine. Using grass seeds and time-lapse photography, Post Typography planted and grew the word 'May', documenting it over the course of three weeks. See a time-lapse animation at their website: *posttypography.com*.

Telekolleg
Piero Glina
This page, bottom: Originally from Germany, Piero Glina is a Zürich-based communication designer. Three-dimensional

letterforms are not always visible at first glance, and this aspect of becoming a camouflaged part of the environment interested Piero. His type experiments in public spaces led to the concept of finding existing grids in urban architecture, which could be used to create a typeface that involved the structure itself. Some words ended up being too big to be photographed entirely. One of the pictures (above, centre, top, right), for example, shows the letters K, O and L from '*Telekolleg*'.

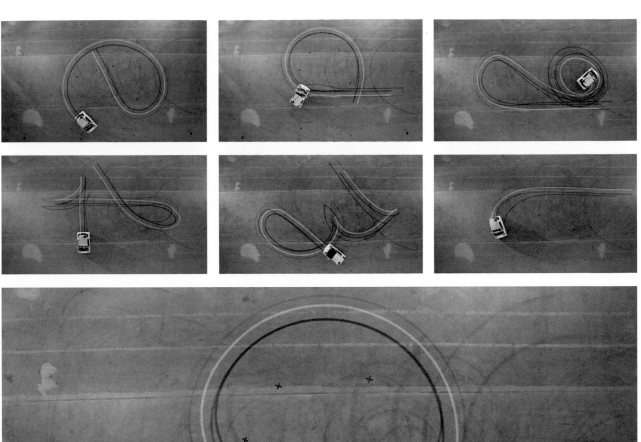

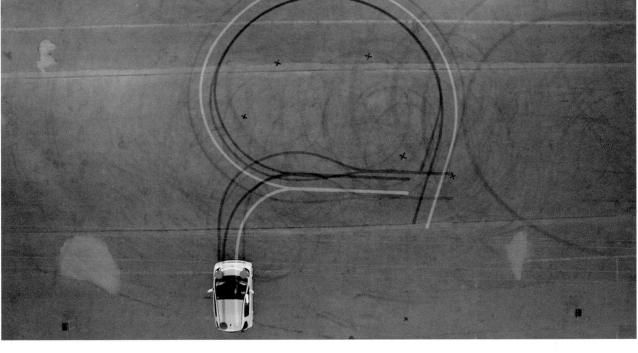

Hello I'm the iQ font

abcdefghijklmnopqrstuvwxyz
ABCDEFGHIJKLMNOPQRSTUVWXYZ
0123456789
. , : : | ? + = @ & ( ) / - # " "

Lorem ipsum dolor sit amet, consectetur adipisicing elit, sed do eiusmod tempor incididunt ut labore et dolore magna aliqua. Ut enim ad minim veniam, quis nostrud exercitation ullamco laboris nisi ut aliquip ex ea commodo consequat. Duis aute irure dolor in reprehenderit in voluptate velit esse cillum dolore eu fugiat nulla pariatur. Excepteur sint occaecat cupidatat non proident, sunt in culpa qui officia deserunt mollit anim id est laborum.

iQ
Pleaseletmedesign

Pleaseletmedesign (PLMD) is a graphic design studio set up in 2004 in Brussels, Belgium, by Pierre Smeets and Damien Aresta. PLMD's friends from the agency Happiness Brussels had the idea of making a font with a car, and invited PLMD to collaborate. First they all sat down with racing driver Stef Van Campenhoudt to discuss the possible car movements. With that information, they tried to visualize how they could obtain a fluid typography on a well-defined surface – as if the car were a pen and Stef the hand. The agency also got interactive artist Zachary Lieberman involved to write software that would let them track the movements of the car in real time. Once a perfect location was found, they installed an HD camera to the ceiling of the hangar. The software was designed to recognize predefined colours in a video and be able to follow the movements of those colours. To follow the movements of the car, they attached four-coloured stickers to its roof. Then everything was carefully choreographed to create the *iQ* typeface in July 2009. The *iQ* font is available as a free download.

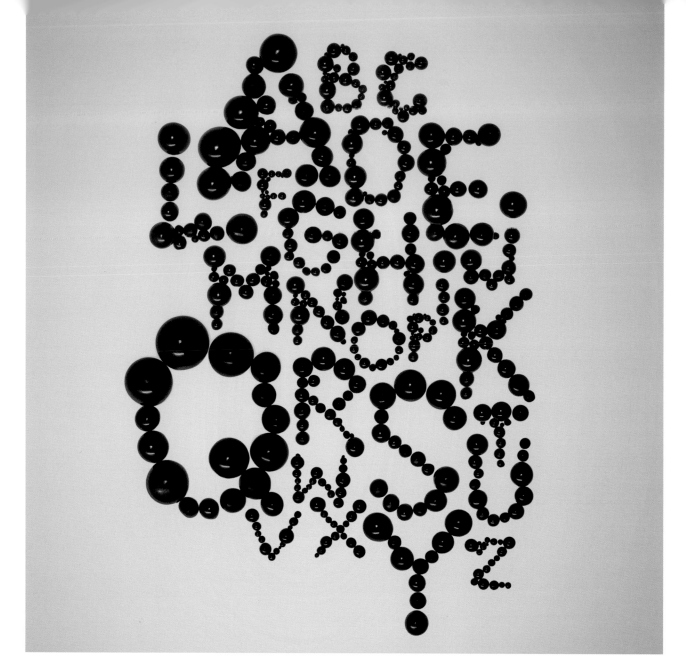

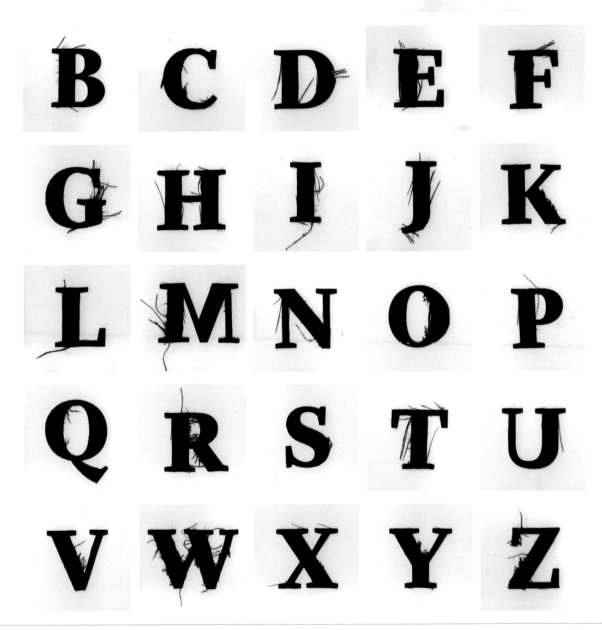

Black Sunday type
Plasticbionic
Left: Animated by his love for arts and typography, French graphic designer Julien Brisson, aka Plasticbionic, has been working freelance since 2004 and since 2006 also at Fly Designers. Inspired by the call for entries to this book, Julien decided he was up for a challenge. He created this three-dimensional alphabet using black balloons ready for the deadline in January 2010.

Fortune Magazine
Peter Crnokrak and Karin von Ompteda
Above: *Fortune Magazine* publishes a yearly special edition on contemporary fashion. For the 2008 edition, they requested custom-designed type that expressed a decidedly 'fashion' aesthetic. In particular, they requested a heavy dark feel that personified the season's style direction. Karin von Ompteda (see also page 136) and Peter Crnokrak of The Luxury of Protest approached the brief by

creating the entire 26 character uppercase set of the magazine's house font, Whitman, in laser-cut black linen. Initial experiments with laser-cutting revealed that if the power of the laser was modulated just below the threshold of fully penetrating through the fabric, a natural fray was produced when they tried to extract the letters from the throwaway surrounding material. Letters were then positioned and scanned at a high resolution to be used in the publication.

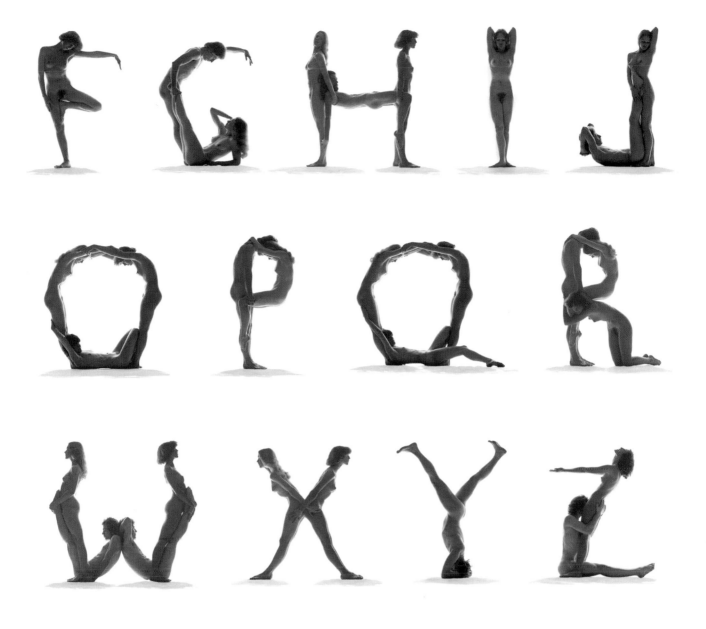

Love Letters
Rowland Scherman

Born in New York in 1937 and now based in Cape Cod, Massachusetts, photographer Rowland Scherman won a Grammy Award in 1968 for his cover for Bob Dylan's *Greatest Hits*. When he was living in London (1970–74), Rowland saw an etching, Giovanni Battista Bracelli's *Alfabeto Figurato*, that showed angels flying around to create the alphabet. He wondered if humans could do that. His studio happened to be next door to Covent Garden Dance Centre, so he asked some performers there if they would like to try. A couple of rehearsals and two days later, the result was *Love Letters*, the first photographic free-standing human typeface ever. '*I tried for a while to make a coffee-table-type book out of it. New York publishers were afraid that the pubes and the Z might offend someone*', Rowland writes. This was in 1975. Later, he showed *Love Letters* in a gallery in Alabama in 1979, and no one so much as complained. Teachers even brought their third-grade students to see it. *Love Letters* has also been exhibited at the Arnolfini Gallery in Bristol and at the Photographer's Gallery in London. After this, the chromes sat in a cupboard for a decade or so. In 2008, Rowland self-published the book *Love Letters – An Anthropomorphic Alphabet*, which is now available online: *blurb.com/bookstore/detail/287269*.

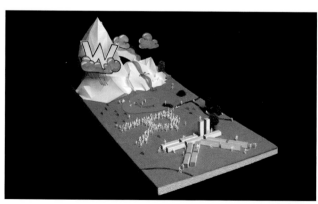

Argento Horror
Brussels
International
Fantastic
Film
Festival

30 June – 5 July 2007
www.bifff.org

Arriscar o Real (Risking Reality)
R2
Left, top: Lizá Ramalho and Artur Rebelo run their design studio R2 in Porto, Portugal. The 'Arriscar o Real' exhibition focused on various artists who explore the mimesis of reality and transform this question into a paradox. Divided into three sections with corresponding spaces, the dominant concept was associated to the meaning of the real and the figurative in space. R2's exhibition design from 2009 was not restricted to a merely informative aspect; it intervened directly in the museum's space. The typography – normally associated with a two-dimensional format – was materialized in the form of a tangible design object. Three-dimensional letters were placed on the entrance hall floor, spelling out the exhibition's name. Photos: Fernando Guerra.

Work
Rebootlab
Left, bottom: Tim Faulwetter and Peter Werner joined forces in 2001 and set up *rebootlab.com*. They are based in Braunschweig, Germany. Their self-initiated installation *Work*, from 2009, sums up how they define inspirational graphic design: a combination of work and play.

Argento Horror
Rafael Farias
Above: Rafael Farias is a London-based graphic designer and artist. Shown here is handmade typography from 2007 that he made for a series of concept posters, promoting a season of horror films by Dario Argento. Argento's films are characterized by a distinctive use of colour, lighting and sound to generate an atmosphere of terror and suspense. The typography consists of string wrapped tightly around a network of nails, reflecting the tension of the films. By adding light, the typography is brought to life, casting an eerie shadow that adds a cinematic quality to the image.

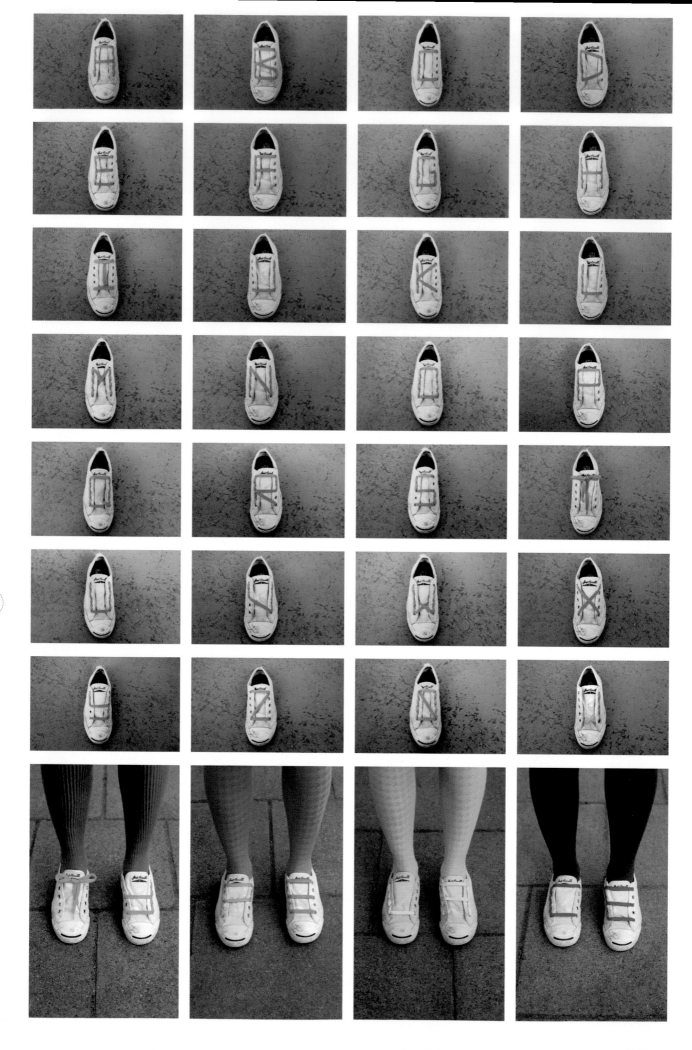

Typelace
Rafael Farias
Left: Designer Rafael Farias is a member of Bumf – an art collective and ongoing online exhibition that involves the creation of work following rules set by the collective. *Typelace* was created in 2009 as a response to a brief set by Bumf: to create a typeface using a single found object. The lace holes on a pair of trainers were used as a grid in order to create the typeface.

The Miracle Worker set
Ryan Molloy
Above: The set for a 2008 performance of *The Miracle Worker* at Chelsea High School, Chelsea, Michigan, was an experiment in including three-dimensional letterforms in the performance itself. Throughout the play, little was done to reveal the typographic nature of the set, focusing more on creating interior and exterior spaces. The climax of the performance is accentuated as the set is transformed to spell the word 'WATER', coinciding with Helen Keller's first successful articulation of the word. Designer: Ryan Molloy; technical theatre director: Ken Faulk; set construction: Chelsea High School Theatre Department.

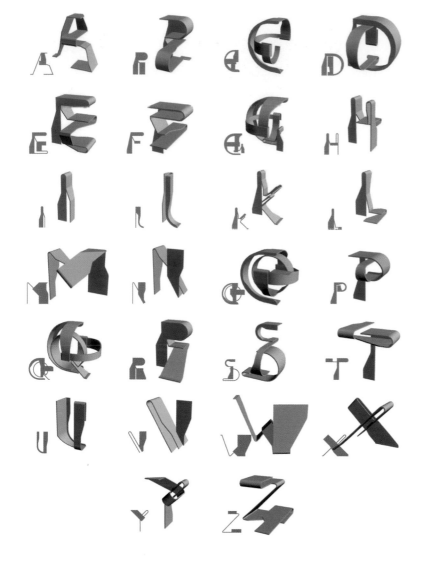
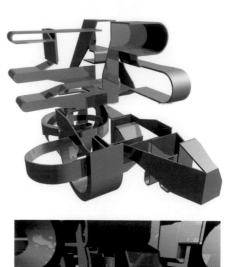

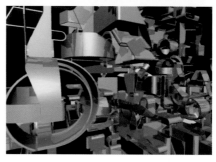

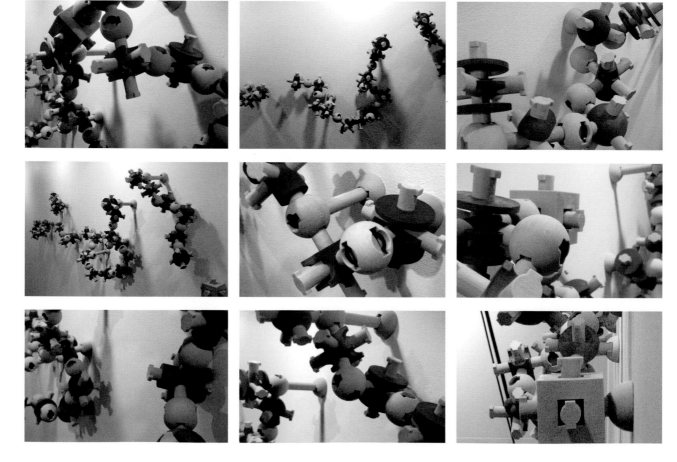

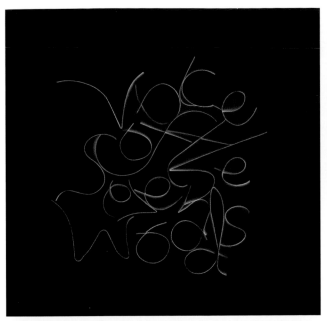

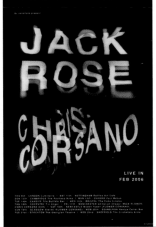

Font-S
Ryan Molloy and Jim Stevens
Left, top: *Font-S* is a dimensional typeface that is modelled on calligraphic two-dimensional typefaces. The ribbon-like planes and forms change in width, emulating pen-tip rotation and brush pressure, looping in on themselves. Individually, the forms of the typeface remain fairly similar to Latin characters, and can be read this way from several vantage points. *Font-S* is typeset in a similar manner to that of written script. Each

letter is connected to each other to form one continuous line using only one rule – no letterform can intersect another. It is really in the typesetting of the typeface that *Font-S* becomes something unique and foreign to what we typically conceive of as dimensional typography. Production assistant: Lindsey Pickornik.

La Robia
Ryan Molloy
Left, bottom: Ryan Molloy collaborated with Jim Stevens to

create *La Robia*, questioning dimensional typography as a structural system. The initial idea was to push beyond traditional conventions and create a system that could ideally be used to construct spaces. Due to material constraints, *La Robia* only exists digitally and as small-scale rapid prototypes of the letterforms.

Various 3D Type Gems
Rick Myers
Above: Rick Myers launched Myers | Art-Utility in 2010, building on commissioned

artwork made since 1996. Shown here are some of Rick's artworks featuring 3D type. From left to right, top to bottom: *Voice of The Seven Woods*, 2008, CDR for Tomlinson; Doves, *Some Cities*, 2005, CD/LP for Doves/ EMI; John Cale, *Turn The Lights On*, 2005, CD for John Cale/ EMI; *Lightning Bolt*, 2005, poster for Flywheel, Easthampton; Chris Corsano, *Jack Rose*, 2006, poster for Corsano. Art direction, design and photography: Rick Myers.

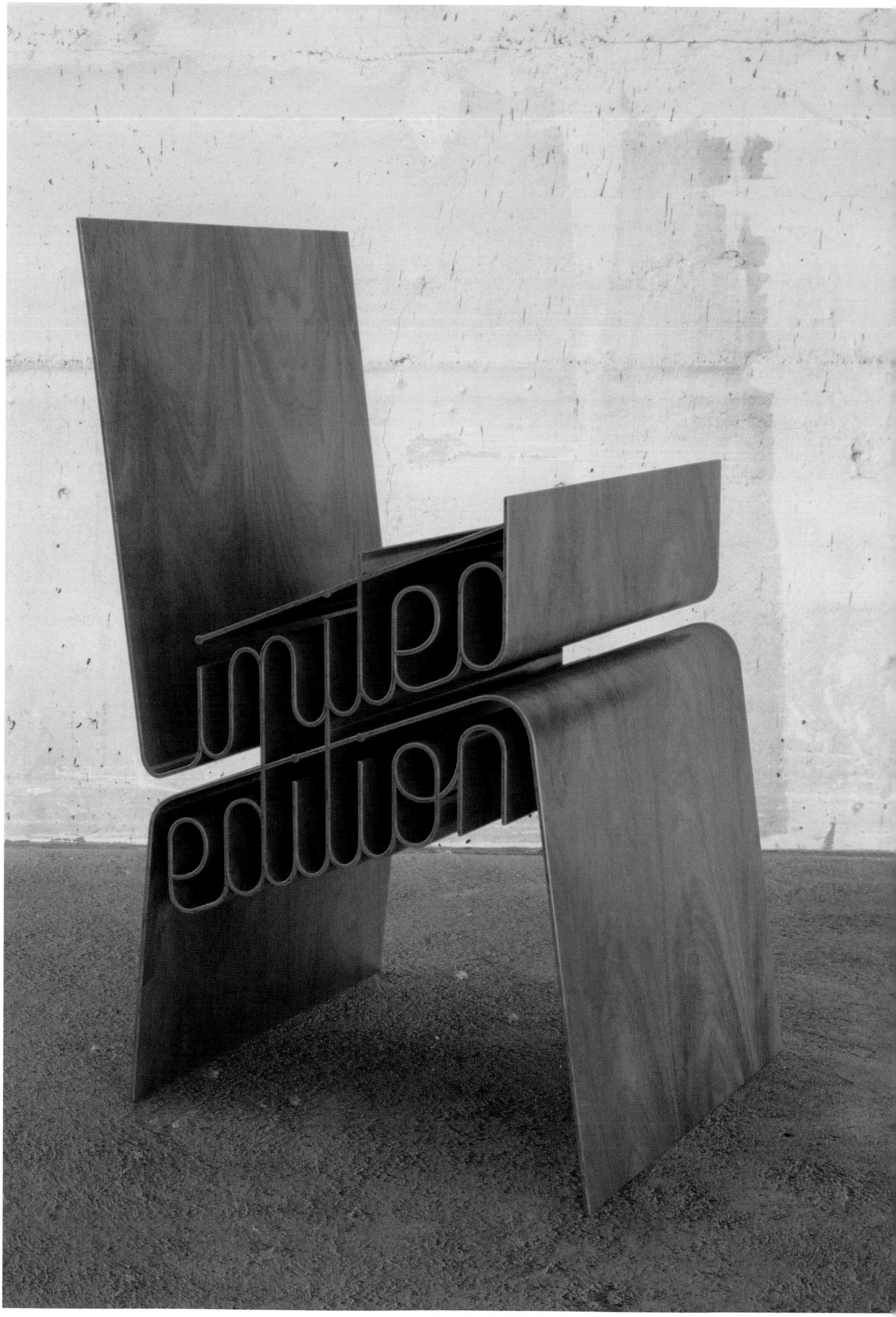

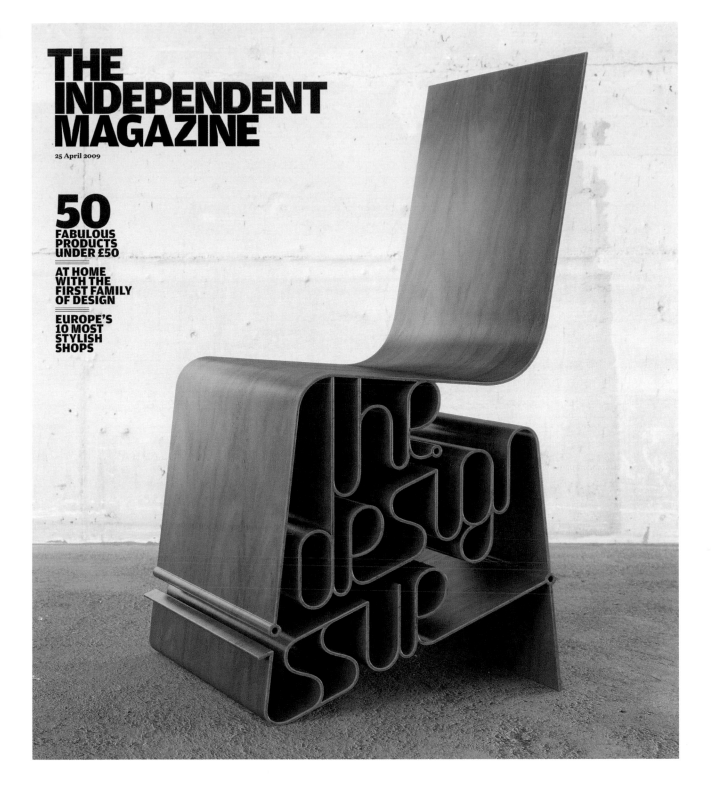

THE INDEPENDENT MAGAZINE

25 April 2009

50
FABULOUS
PRODUCTS
UNDER £50

AT HOME
WITH THE
FIRST FAMILY
OF DESIGN

EUROPE'S
10 MOST
STYLISH
SHOPS

Limited Edition

Rinzen

Left: The Australian art and design group Rinzen is perhaps best known for the collaborative approach of its five members, formed as a result of their *RMX* project in 2000. *Limited Edition*, from 2008, was created for the cover of the book *Limited Edition: Prototypes, One-Offs and Design Art Furniture*, written by Sophie Lovell and published by Birkhäuser Verlag. Design and art direction were by Rinzen's Steve Alexander. The *Limited Edition* display typeface was designed and reconfigured in the shape of a chair by Steve Alexander; the final image was rendered by Rune Spanns.

The Design Issue

Rinzen

Above: Shown here is the cover of the UK's *The Independent Magazine's* design issue from 2009, featuring the *Limited Edition* book. Design and art direction were by Rinzen's Steve Alexander. *The Design Issue* display typeface was designed and reconfigured in the shape of a chair by Steve Alexander at Rinzen; the final image was also rendered by Rune Spanns.

Alphabottes

Raphaël Legrand

Paris-based graphic designer Raphaël Legrand avoids working with his computer whenever he can. His three-dimensional typeface, *Alphabottes*, is a good example of the lengths to which he goes to achieve this goal. *Alphabottes* was a part of Raphaël's final-year project at ESAAB in Nevers, France, from where he graduated in 2002. The project dealt with the image of the agricultural world. After 2002, *Alphabottes* was displayed once more at an exhibition in 2004 that took place in Paris. The typeface is based on a pixel-like grid of three by five hay bales – with the exception of a few wider letters. This is a particularly physical way to go about typesetting, especially when exposed to the weather.

Nature

Sean Martindale

Left: Sean Martindale is an interdisciplinary artist and designer currently residing in Toronto. His interventions activate public and semi-public spaces to encourage engagement, frequently focused on ecological and social issues. Installed in spring 2009, *Nature* was the first part of an ongoing project. For this intervention, Sean crafted large individual 3D letters (1.2 m/4 ft high x 0.45 m/1.5 ft deep) to spell out the word 'NATURE' using salvaged scraps of cardboard. He then left these letters anonymously on the curb alongside regular garbage and recycling bins in Toronto. The letters were subsequently picked up and crushed by one of the city's organic waste and recycling trucks. The project was documented both photographically and on video.

Free

Sean Martindale

Above: Following *Nature*, in 2009 The Art Gallery of Ontario kindly lent Sean the use of its parking lot for his next project. The lot is a fenced-off enclosure that bisects Butterfield Park and Grange Park in the downtown Toronto core. Over the years, ownership and use of the site have been highly contested. Besides commenting on these structures and the site itself, Sean also chose the word 'FREE' in reference to the public aspect of his practice. In the end, more than 6.6 km (21,663 ft) of salvaged string was used – two high-tension lengths for each of the 231 points/nodes crossing the 13.4 m (44 ft) distance between the fences, plus the letter outlines.

Currency
Sean Martindale

Left, top: This temporary project was installed in conjunction with an educational fundraising event organized by Sean Martindale in 2008 for Haliburton Community Organic Farm in Victoria, British Columbia, Canada. To create the piece, he gathered over 6,000 plastic water bottles. The piece was installed adjacent to a municipal water facility. The bottles were inserted into the chain-link fence surrounding the water facility to spell 'currency'.

Park
Sean Martindale

Left, bottom: In 2009, Sean used salvaged turf to spell out the word 'PARK' with grass in an empty parking lot in downtown Toronto. The space is next to a busy street, surrounded by tall buildings and other pay-parking spaces. There is a lack of plants and green spaces in the area, and for some time the parking lot had been empty aside from mud, waste and strewn garbage. Local residents, workers and visitors to the area have warmly

welcomed the unsolicited addition and it has become a favourite sight in the neighbourhood. He was assisted by Joe Clement, who returned to water the project on several occasions for lack of rain. Grass is resilient, so the project should keep growing and take root until/ unless somebody removes it.

TSE
Sebastian Lemm

Above: Independent graphic designer Sebastian Lemm, a native of Germany, relocated to New York City in 2000 after graduating from Berlin University of the Arts. Sebastian created this installation while still in art school. He was interested in issues of legibility on the page as well as in space and the perception of information.

S

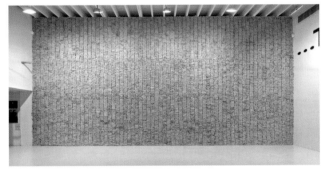

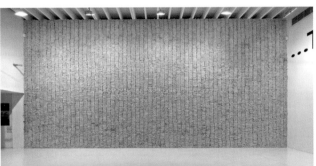

Everything I Do Always Comes Back to Me
Sagmeister Inc.
Left, top: Stefan Sagmeister formed Sagmeister Inc. in New York in 1993. Apart from commissioned work, his studio also works on self-initiated projects. Shown here are six double-page spreads from 2002 made for *Austrian Magazine*. Art direction: Stefan Sagmeister; designers: Stefan Sagmeister, Eva Hueckmann, Doris Pesendorfer and Matthias Ernstberger, who also took

the pictures; modelmaking: Eva Hueckmann; backgrounds ('everything', 'to me'): Wolf-Gordon.

Having Guts Always Works Out for Me
Sagmeister Inc.
Left, centre: Six double-page spreads from 2003 made for *Austrian Magazine*. Art direction and design: Stefan Sagmeister, Matthias Ernstberger and Miao Wang; photos: Bela Borsodi. (See also page 44.)

Trying to Look Good Limits My Life
Sagmeister Inc.
Left, bottom: Five visuals created in 2004 for *Art Grandeur Nature*. The title of this work (and its content) is among the things that Stefan has learned in his life. They were displayed in sequence as typographic billboards – like sentimental greeting cards – and left in a park north of Paris. Art direction and design: Stefan Sagmeister and Matthias Ernstberger, who also took the pictures.

Banana Wall
Sagmeister Inc.
Above: At the 2008 opening of an exhibition at Deitch Projects in New York, Sagmeister Inc. featured a wall of 10,000 bananas. Green bananas created a pattern against a background of yellow bananas spelling out 'Self-confidence produces fine results'. After a few days, the green bananas turned yellow too and the type disappeared. Art direction: Stefan Sagmeister; design: Richard The and Joe Shouldice.

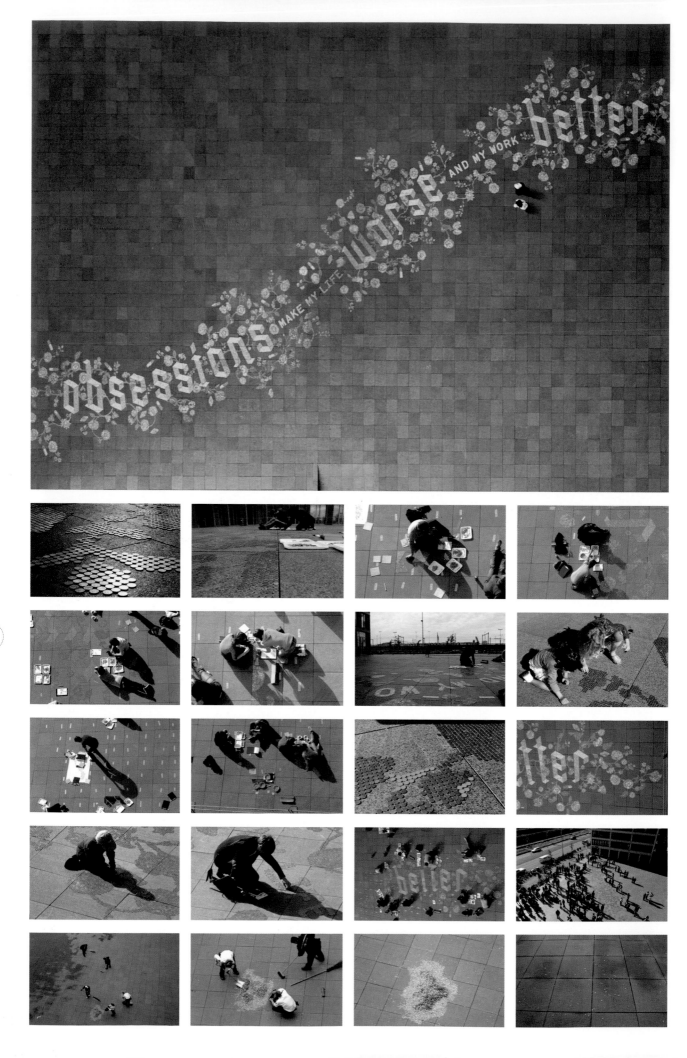

Obsessions Make My Life Worse and My Work Better

Sagmeister Inc.

Left: On 13 September 2008, Sagmeister Inc. began the installation of 250,000 Euro cents on Waagdragerhof Square in Amsterdam. Over the course of eight days, and with the help of more than 100 volunteers, the coins were sorted into four different shades and carefully placed over a 300 sq m (3,230 sq ft) area, according to a master plan. After completion, the coins were left free and unguarded for the public to interact with. Within 20 hours after the installation's opening, local residents noticed a person bagging the coins and taking them away. Protective of the design piece they had watched being created, they called the police. After stopping the 'criminal', the police – in an effort to 'preserve the artwork' – swept up every remaining cent and carted the coins away. Art direction: Stefan Sagmeister; design: Richard The and Joe Shouldice; photos: Jens Rehr and Dennis de Groot.

Vilcek Prize trophy

Sagmeister Inc.

This page, top: This Vilcek Prize award trophy was created in 2005 for a major new award programme honouring the outstanding achievements of foreign-born Americans within the fields of the visual arts and biomedical research. Art direction: Stefan Sagmeister; design: Stefan Sagmeister and Matthias Ernstberger; 3D consulting: Nick Herman; 3D design: Aly Khalifa.

Vilcek Creative Promise certificate

Sagmeister Inc.

This page, bottom: This certificate, designed in 2009, comprises three layers of intricately laser-die-cut paper. When hung for display, the neon orange back side of the paper reflects on itself and the wall, making it appear as though it is glowing. Creative direction: Stefan Sagmeister; design: Joe Shouldice for the Vilcek Foundation; production: BlackBooks Stencils.

The Happy Film
Sagmeister Inc.
Left, top: Shown here are video stills from some of the title sequences of Sagmeister's self-initiated *The Happy Film*. At the time of editing this book, the film, on Sagmeister's attempts to find happiness, was still being shot. It has so far taken him to remote parts of Indonesia and even happiness conferences.

Black String
Sveta Sebyakina
Left, bottom: Sveta is a graphic designer, type designer and art director at Republica design studio in Moscow. She has created hundreds of handmade 3D typefaces for her project *8:00 Good Morning*. One of them is her experimental typeface and font *Black String*, which was created in 2009.

Skin
Shotopop
Above: Created in 2010 by London-based Casper Franken and Carin Standford of Shotopop, these letterforms are cleverly constructed using negative space. The black shapes were cut out of foamboard and propped up on light stands or suspended from the backdrop stand. As the shapes are not on the same level, they only form the word 'SKIN' when viewed from a certain angle. This photograph is part of a set of five images that Shotopop made for the artist Skin, but is the only one of the series that featured typography. Art direction, design, set build and photography: Shotopop; lighting: Matthew Halls and Natasha Alipour-Faridani (Garage Studios); styling: Kim Howells; make-up: Kirstin Piggott; model: SKIN; client: SKIN.

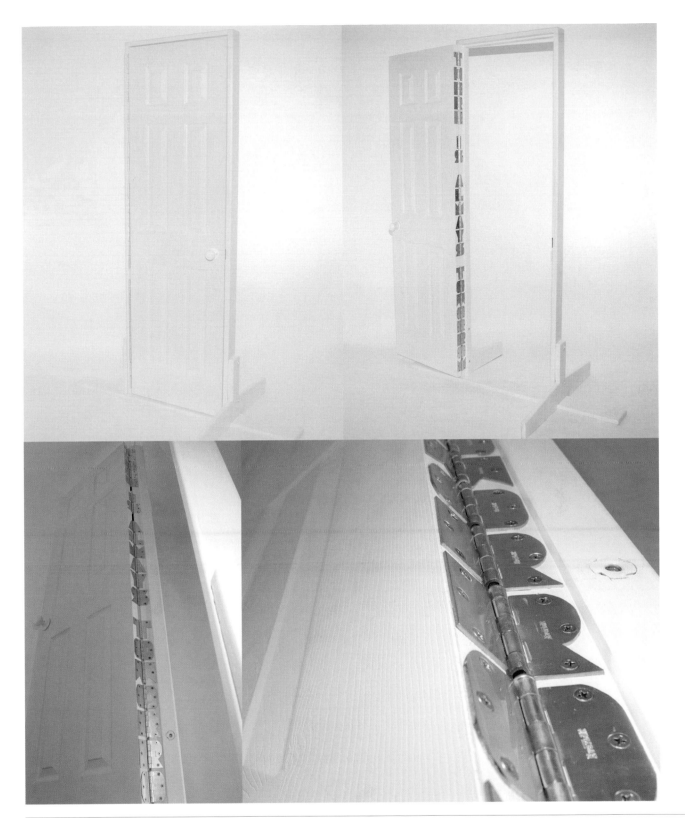

Mech Type
Sebastian Gagin

Left, top: Born and raised in Buenos Aires, Argentina, graphic designer Sebastian Gagin graduated in 2009 from the University of Buenos Aires. *Mech Type* was created using the Meccano Steel-Tec game that his father gave him when he was eight years old. Years later, Sebastian rediscovered the game in his cupboard and started playing.

Smashed Up
Siobhan Tarr

Left, centre: Freelance mosaic artist Siobhan Tarr was born and grew up in England. She then lived in Australia before moving to Germany, where she now lives in the countryside between Hamburg and Luebeck. This A–Z is made up of smashed cups and plates, predominantly white porcelain but here and there a patterned shard is thrown in for good luck. In Germany, they say that *'smashed porcelain brings good luck'*, and on an evening before a wedding the guests are invited to come laden down with old cups and plates for a smashing happening.

IDEA
Sharon Pazner

Left, bottom: Artist and architect Sharon Pazner grew up in the USA and studied in France and Israel, where she now works from her Tel Aviv studio. One of her many typographic pieces is *IDEA*, which was created using paper that Sharon then scanned.

Hinge
Satsuki Atsumi

Above: A pupil of Andrew Byrom, Satsuki Atsumi was born in Shizuoka, Japan, and moved to California in 2004, where she graduated from California State University, Long Beach. *Hinge* was designed there in 2010.

Minimal Bloc
Superscript²
Left, top: Graphic design studio
Superscript² was founded by
Pierre Delmas Bouly and Patrick
Lallemand in 2006 in Lyon,
France. Their self-initiated
Minimal Bloc type, from
2006/07, is composed of
simple geometric shapes.
Each letter of the alphabet
has several drawings.

Type at the Beach
Studio Xavier Encinas
Left, centre: Xavier Encinas is
a French art director living and
working in Paris, France. Xavier
assembled and photographed
these letters during his holidays
in 2008 at the Sunshine Coast,
British Columbia, Canada.

Monday
Start
Left, bottom: Start is a collective;
the vision of Phil Robson and
Mat Carlot. Originally from
London and Paris, they met in

Sydney, Australia. They created
this series of self-initiated
3D type experiments using
laser-cut, black and mirrored
acrylic and also a laser-etch for
further treatments.

Loudmouth
Start
Above: Dope! Word! FFFresh!
Safe! These three-dimensional
comic book explosions were the
first collaboration between Phil
Robson and Mat Carlot. The
duo designed them digitally
first, then laser-cut and etched

them onto 3 mm (⅛ in) sheets
of ply. Phil created the typeform
and graphic shapes, while Mat
created his signature pattern
as repeat texture to the piece.
The pieces are available via
the team's website,
thebrandnewstart.com, and
measure approximately
50 x 40 x 3 cm (19 x 15 x 1 in).

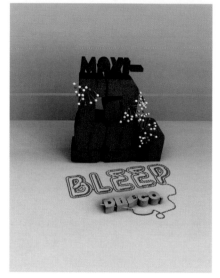

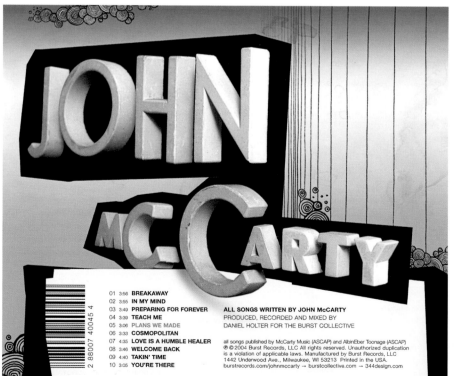

01 3:56 **BREAKAWAY**
02 3:55 **IN MY MIND**
03 3:49 **PREPARING FOR FOREVER**
04 3:39 **TEACH ME**
05 3:06 **PLANS WE MADE**
06 3:33 **COSMOPOLITAN**
07 4:35 **LOVE IS A HUMBLE HEALER**
08 3:46 **WELCOME BACK**
09 4:40 **TAKIN' TIME**
10 3:05 **YOU'RE THERE**

ALL SONGS WRITTEN BY JOHN McCARTY

PRODUCED, RECORDED AND MIXED BY
DANIEL HOLTER FOR THE BURST COLLECTIVE

2 88007 40045 4

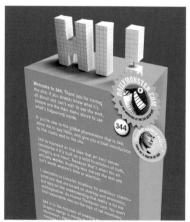

John McCarty
plans we made

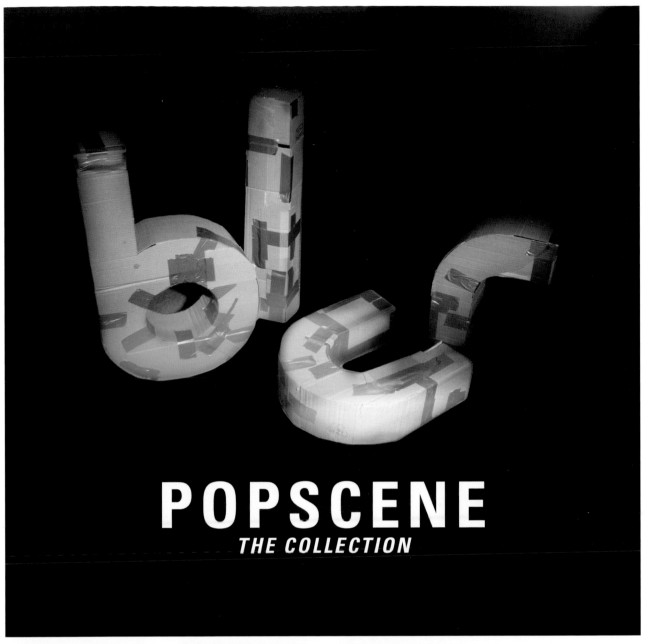

POPSCENE
THE COLLECTION

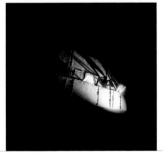

Ministry of Sound: Genres
Studio Output
Left, top: UK-based Studio
Output was set up in 2002 by
Rob Coke, Dan Moore and Ian
Hambleton. These images,
scribbled with felt-tip pens, were
commissioned by the Ministry of
Sound to advertise their quarterly
Saturday Sessions radio shows.
They celebrate the diversity in
the many subgenres of music.
Design: Stewart McMillan.

John McCarty
Stefan G. Bucher, 344 Design
Left, bottom, left: Stefan G.
Bucher runs the design studio
344 Design. In 2004, indie artist
John McCarty needed a visual
calling card. Stefan created a
portrait of him based on photos
by Peter Batchelder and Nathan
Harrmann. The main type was set
with clay display letters that
Stefan bought at a flea market.

344design.com's Hi!
Stefan G. Bucher, 344 Design
Left, bottom, right: Stefan
believes in manners, so he
wanted to make sure his site
actually says 'hello' before
anything else. Aesthetically, he
wanted to let people know right
away that the 344 Empire is
located at the intersection of
the homespun and the epic.

Blur box
Stylorouge
This page, top and bottom, left:
Shown here are a few of the lo-fi
proposals for the latest Blur *Best
of* album sleeve. Aaron Munday
constructed them at London-
based consultancy Stylorouge.

Livan
Stylorouge
This page, bottom, centre
and right: 3D metalwork type
created for the musician Livan.
Designed and constructed by
Aaron Munday.

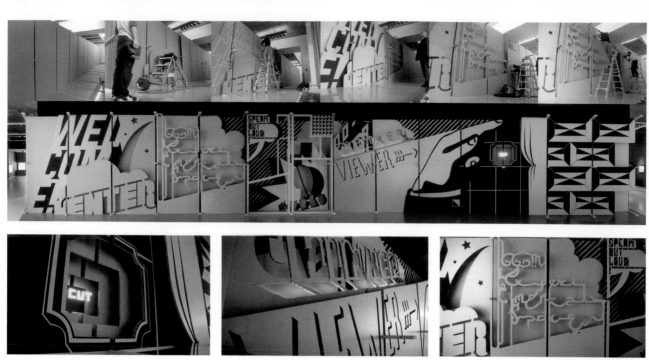

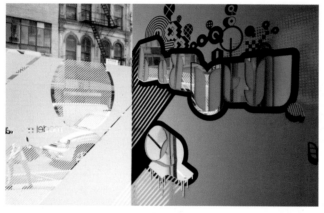

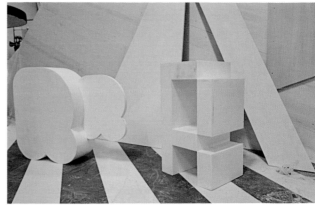

Big Type Says More
Strange Attractors Design
Left, top: Strange Attractors Design is run by Ryan Pescatore Frisk and Catelijne van Middelkoop in Rotterdam, the Netherlands and in New York City. In 2006, the team manually produced a typographic installation, more than 17 m (55 ft) wide, as part of the ongoing exhibition 'Cut for Purpose', at Museum Boijmans van Beuningen in Rotterdam. The piece is now part of the museum's permanent collection.

Q
Strange Attractors Design
Left, centre: In 2008, Q Model Management in the USA approached Strange Attractors to create a custom typographic installation, for the interior as well as the windows, that would integrate with the architecture of their new street-level office on Broadway, Manhattan. Using laser-cut mirror and custom vinyl, the text by poet Kahlil Gibran says: *'Beauty is eternity gazing at itself in the mirror'.*

Truman
Supermundane
Left, bottom: Supermundane is the pseudonym of London-based designer Rob Lowe. The *Truman* font was literally staring him in the face for years; he always loved the way this iconic architectural gem (the Truman Brewery) dominated and gave an identity to the area of Brick Lane in east London. The main reason Rob designed the *Truman* font was because he couldn't believe nobody else had and it seemed to be crying out to be made.

Letterlab
Strange Attractors Design
Above: Installed at the Graphic Design Museum Breda, the Netherlands, between October 2009 and January 2011, 'Letterlab' was an exhibition created for children aged between 6 and 13. 'Letterlab' offered playful exploration and discovery of letters, their sounds, meaning and shape. Strange Attractors were responsible for the exhibition's 2D, 3D, multimedia and type design.

STUPOR

ABCDEFGHIJKLM
NOPQRSTUVWXYZ

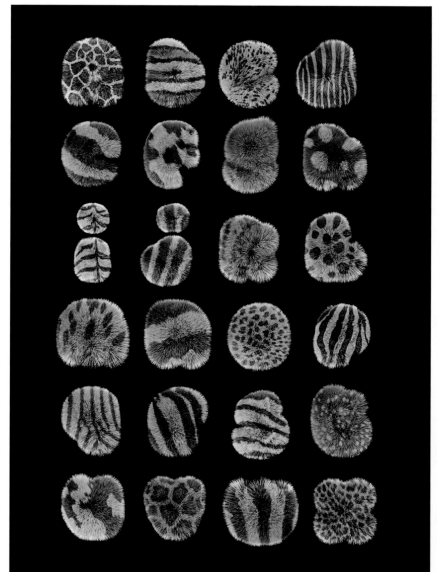  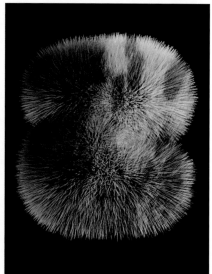

Stupor
Sakis Kyratzis
Left, top: Sakis Kyratzis is a designer, photographer and interaction designer working mainly with architects and the cultural sector. *Stupor* uses the folds and creases in fabric to create letterforms. The alphabet was created using translucent silk fabric that was then photographed on a lightbox. As a result, the letters have an almost liquid quality.

Fat and Furry
Sean Freeman
Left, bottom: Sean Freeman is a typographic enthusiast, with the majority of his work being semi-photographic. *Fat and Furry*, from 2009, is an experiment into making a typeface that was as fat and as furry as possible.

Medicine Capsule alphabet
Simone Stecher
Above: Simone Stecher grew up in South Tyrol in Italy and studied graphic design at the University of Wales, Newport. Her *Medicine Capsule* alphabet started as a university project. Students were asked to create a 3D typeface that clearly expressed the inherent characteristics of the material they were assigned. Simone's material was medication (pills and tablets). She experimented with putting medicine capsules into a letter-shaped ice-cube tray and pouring hot water over them. The capsules broke up and dissolved, releasing the liquid medicine inside them. The frozen letters were then placed on white paper, where they melted beautifully.

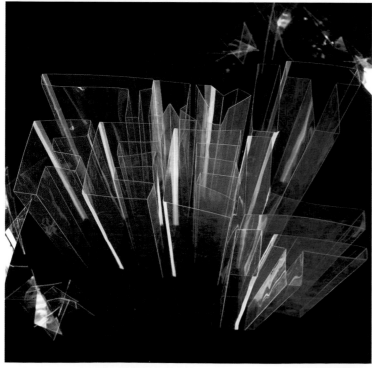

ABCDE
FGHIJK
LMNOP
QRSTU
VWXY

Tasty Bytes CD covers
s3studio
Left: Graphic designer Maxime Archambault runs Montreal-based s3studio. He created these two CD covers for *Start,* by Omni, and *Try It Feel It,* by Nite Cells, both released by Los Angeles-based Tasty Bytes Records.

One Hundred And
Studio Lundsager
Above: London-based Studio Lundsager is run by designer and art director Mikkel Lundsager Hansen. *One Hundred And* was created during his Masters degree at Central Saint Martins College in London. To create the title sequence and DVD menu for a narrative project with a handmade feel that he was working on, Mikkel consulted his father Jörgen Hansen, a ceramic artist. In his father's workshop, Mikkel carved out

letterforms in clay. After they dried, they were put in a kiln and heated to about 1,000°C (1,832°F). While still glowing hot, the letterforms were taken out of the kiln and placed on the ground, where the shades of grey and black appeared as a result of the cooling process. The process of creating the letters became part of the title sequence as well as the letters themselves.

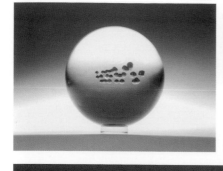
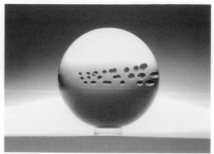
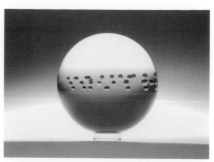
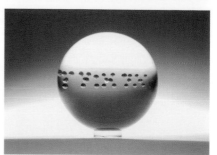
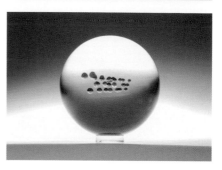
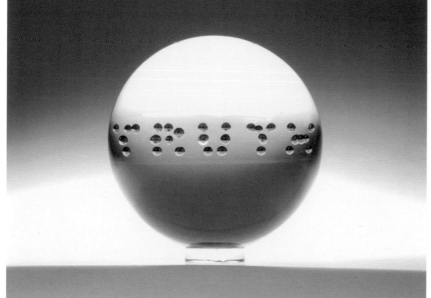

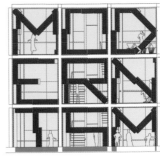

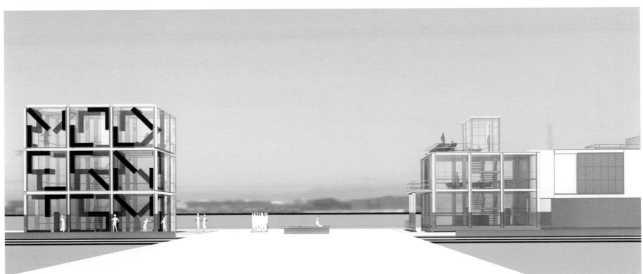

The Truth
Studio for Virtual Typography
Left, top: This typographic sculpture was created by Matthias Hillner of the Studio for Virtual Typography. Thirty chrome-plated balls are embedded in clear resin spheres, measuring 20 cm (7 in) across. The reflective balls give shape to the word 'TRUTH' when seen from one particular angle. The three-dimensional nature of the silver spheres, as well as the distorting effect of the surrounding material makes *The Truth* look more or less obscure depending on the viewing angle.

Sculptura
Studio for Virtual Typography
Left, bottom: *Sculptura* was inspired by a sculptural sketch that Picasso had created in tribute to the writer Guillaume Apollinaire. While visiting a Picasso exhibition, Matthias was reminded of a typographic scribble that he had once made as a bored schoolboy. Faced with Picasso's work, Matthias wondered how the diagonal lines in his scribble would feel when projected into three dimensions. While rendering a digital version of *Sculptura*, he explored the font physically by casting it in resin. Depending on the viewing angle, the letters are more or less recognizable.

Updating Modernism
Studio for Virtual Typography
Above: *Updating Modernism* was a joint project between former Pentagram colleagues Matthias Hillner and Zlatko Haban. Zlatko invited Matthias to help design an exhibition pavilion for the Bauhaus site in Dessau. The pavilion was planned to be placed where the former Gropius house had stood until it was replaced by a traditional German architecture. The design of their pavilion was based on the Cubico typeface, which was used to spell the word 'Modernism'. Even though the pavilion was never built, the design solution was displayed during an exhibition in Weimar in 2006.

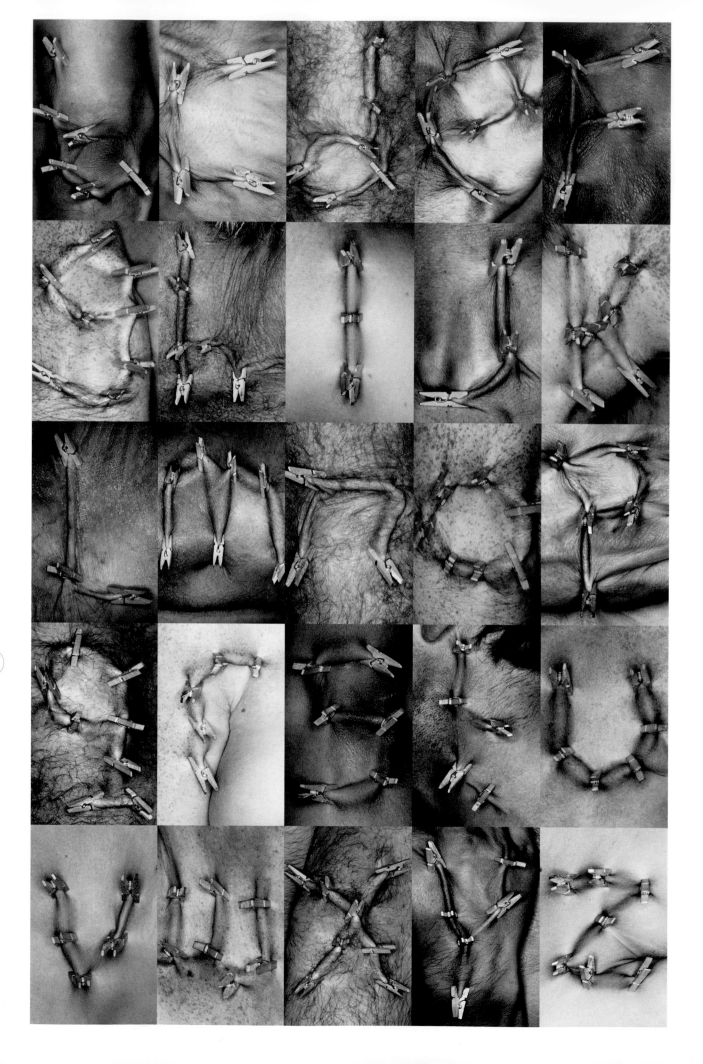

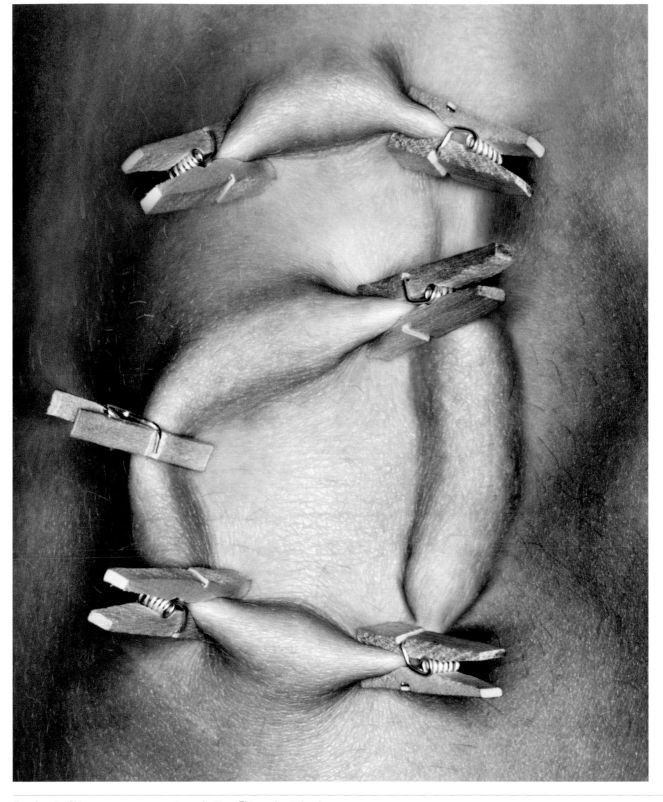

Typeface in Skin
Thijs Verbeek
Thijs Verbeek lives and works
in Amsterdam as a designer
for commissioned and self-
initiated projects. Between
2006 and 2008, he created
this provocative alphabet
using clothes pegs and skin. It
generates very mixed feelings.
Every letter has its own character
when applied because of the
use of skin and various skin
types: flexible skin results in
voluptuous shapes, while taut
skin gives the letter a sense of
imperfection. This makes it hard
to predict the final shape. The
clothes pegs are more than just
a tool for keeping the folds in
place. Photos: Arjan Benning.

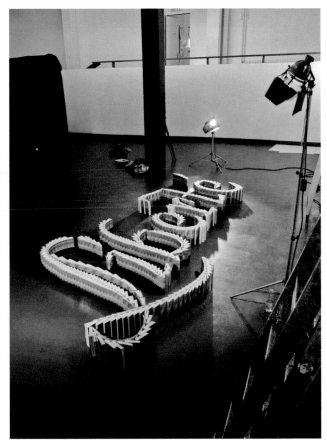

Good Times – Informe
Underware's Type Workshop
Left, top: Pan-European design collective Underware was founded in 1999 by Akiem Helmling, Bas Jacobs and Sami Kortemäki. They are based in Den Haag, Helsinki and Amsterdam. Underware regularly conducts type workshops. Shown here are a few pictures from the 'Good Times' workshop held in Florence, Italy, which took place in December 2005. From the ground floor, the final 3D installation looked like an illegible, mysterious yet fascinating architectural sculpture. From the top floor, however, the lettering could clearly be read. In Italian, *'informe'* means 'without form', but the word was also meant to suggest the English verb 'inform'. More than 300 sq m (3,230 sq ft) of Marazzi tiles were used to create this temporary installation.

Moveable Type
Underware's Type Workshop
Left, bottom: 'Moveable Type' – a celebration of manual work – was a one-day type workshop held in the vast space of the historic buildings of the Waterschei coal mine, close to Genk, Belgium, in 2005. The modules they used were empty cardboard boxes.

Manual Pixelism – Liberté
Underware's Type Workshop
Above: This type workshop, entitled 'Manual Pixelism', was held in Lausanne, Switzerland, in 2005. It resulted in two particularly exciting and widely published pieces: *Liberté* (freedom), seen here, and *Dream On* (shown overleaf). The team were lucky to get their hands on 300 books of the same edition to play with. The fact that the books have identical sizes enhances the sheer beauty and simplicity of this piece.

Manual Pixelism – Dream
Underware's Type Workshop
Top: Following the *Liberté* piece shown on the previous page, here is another very successful result of the 'Manual Pixelism' workshop. With hundreds of supermarket trolleys at their disposal, and a big car park as their canvas, the team worked for several days to produce this piece, including a very long, cold winter's night with temperatures around a painful –8°C (17°F).

Darkmark – Utopia
Underware's Type Workshop
Left, bottom: Underware held a four-day workshop in June 2008 at the Otis College of Art and Design, Los Angeles, focusing on shadow and light. The resulting typographic installations ended up being particularly poetic. This bizarre-looking installation, for instance, resembles a spider's web with an obscure catch. The shadow says it all – but only at 11.30 in the morning.

Darkmark – Go Away
Underware's Type Workshop
This page, bottom: Another intriguing example from the shadow type workshop. This controlled yet chaotic collection of wood resembling fencing sends a very clear message.

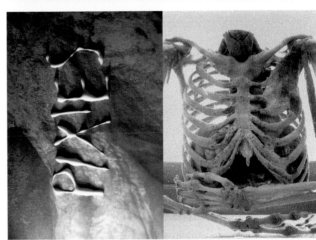

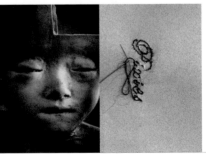

Minotaur

Vaughan Oliver

Vaughan is best known for the body of work he created for UK-based music label 4AD. The label's identity was designed in 1980 and was maintained by Oliver and his collaborators for 25 years. This body of work included the now-classic record sleeves for influential rock band The Pixies. The five 4AD releases from The Pixies were reissued as both limited edition and deluxe edition collectors' sets in 2009 entitled *Minotaur*. Vaughan was commissioned by Jeff Anderson, founder of A+R (Artist in Residence), to revisit the designs. Working with some of his students, and reunited with Pixies photographer Simon Larbalestier, Vaughan reinterpreted the artwork. Shown here are a few sample spreads from the oversized *Minotaur* hardcover book. The deluxe edition of the set includes all five Pixies studio albums – *Come On Pilgrim* (1987), *Surfer Rosa* (1988), *Doolittle* (1989), *Bossanova* (1990) and *Trompe le Monde* (1991) – on 24k layered CD and Blu-ray, with all the new artwork. Also included in the deluxe edition is a DVD of a 1991 performance at the Brixton Academy in London, the group's videos, live tracks, and a 54-page book, all in a custom slipcase. The limited edition version includes everything in the deluxe edition as well as all five albums on 180g vinyl, a Giclée print of Vaughan's artwork, and a 72-page hardcover book, in an oversized custom clamshell cover.

Art direction and design: Vaughan Oliver; photos: Simon Larbalestier; contributing students from UCA, Epsom: Rosie Upright, Phoebe Richardson, Rose Thomas, Ben Ewing and Aaron Kitney.

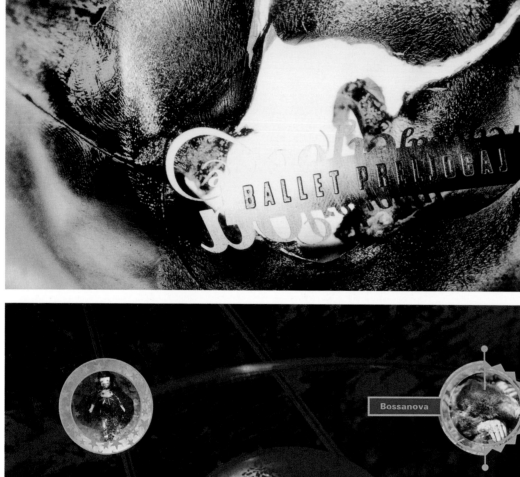

MODERN *Calendar* '96

96

𝒲
(23)

conceived and compiled by vaughan oliver at v23

contributions from   colin gray

jim friedman

michele turriani

cohen / slatoff

chris bigg

simon larbalestier

jason love

paul mcmenamin

olga norman / nicola schwartz

adrian philpott (tom croes)

dominic davies

vaughan oliver (ichiro kono)

adrian taylor

May

"it seems to me that a calendar
is for letting you know where you're at."

VULVA O'REIGHAN
editor, this rimy river

Dedicated to T *leaf* Morley

Originated and printed in England by Botany Lithographic, Tonbridge, Kent

CAL. Nº. (Minty 23)

Ballet Preljocaj
Vaughan Oliver
Left, top: Identity for dance
company Ballet Preljocaj from
1997. Art direction: Vaughan
Oliver; design: Vaughan Oliver
and Tim Vary.

Bossanova
Vaughan Oliver
Left, bottom: Iconic front cover
of the Pixies album *Bossanova*,
released in 1990. Credits:
Art direction and design:
Vaughan Oliver; photo: Simon
Larbalestier; modelmaking:

Pirate; design assistance:
Chris Bigg.

Modern Calendar '96
Vaughan Oliver
Top: This calendar by v23 was
conceived, art directed and
designed by Vaughan Oliver. The
cover photography is by Chris
Bigg. Contributing photographers
featured here on the top right
are Michele Turriani (March;
model: Maya), Chris Bigg (May)
and Paul McMenamin (August).

Beggars Banquet
Vaughan Oliver
Bottom, left and centre: This
identity from 2000 for record
companies' group Beggars
Group was commissioned by
Martin Mills. Art direction:
Vaughan Oliver; modelmaking:
Adrian Taylor; photos: Martin
Andersen; design: Tim Vary.

Satellite
Vaughan Oliver
Bottom, right: Commissioned by
Julia Reed and Satellite Films,
this identity for Satellite was

created in 1994. Art direction:
Vaughan Oliver; modelmaking:
Adrian Taylor; photos: Tom Croes;
design: Kees Hubers.

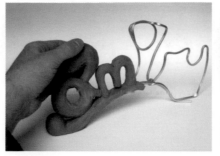

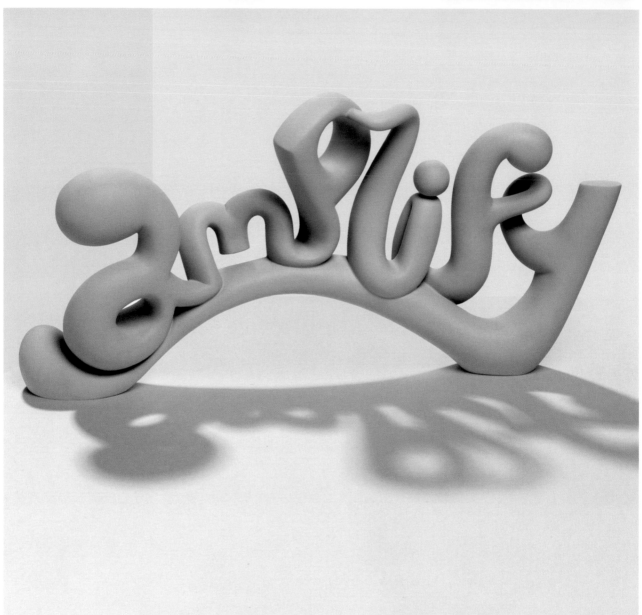

Amplify
Wilfrid Wood
Left: Following his graduation from Central Saint Martins, London, Wilfrid Wood worked for the TV programme *Spitting Image* as a head builder (the satirical programme featured caricature puppets of public figures). Nowadays, Wilfrid does almost entirely commissioned or self-initiated 3D work, creating heads, figures and some lettering using polymer clay, aluminium armature wire, an airbrush and loads of sandpaper. The brief for the *Amplify* logo shown here was completely open-ended; they liked the lettering experiments Wilfrid had made for himself and wanted something similar.
Client: Amplify – Experiential Marketing Agency; art direction: Carlos Fitzpatrick.

Stackers
Wilfrid Wood
This page, top: *Stackers* is a logo for a range of bathroom toys. The brief was to come up with something 'watery'!
Client: Pentagram; art direction: Jane Pluer.

Various
Wilfrid Wood
This page, bottom: The various pieces below the Stackers lettering are all self-initiated.

A

Adam Voorhes
voorhes.com
A 21
Photographer Adam Voorhes is a graduate from Brooks Institute, Santa Barbara, California, USA. He first moved to Los Angeles, then to New York. Adam now works in his own studio in Austin, Texas, USA, where he enjoys life with his wife and dogs.

Akatre
akatre.com
A 18, A 19, A 20
Akatre was founded by Valentin Abad, Julien Dhivert and Sebastien Riveron. The partners met at art college and the idea of Akatre was born there. However, the studio's launch was delayed for a year while all three partners gained experience at other studios and companies, including Philippe Apeloig, Integral Ruedi Baur, Pyramyd Editions, Michel Bouvet and Aer' studio. Valentin, Julien and Sebastien then joined forces to set up their own independent studio close to Paris.

Alex Robbins
alexrobbins.co.uk
A 27
Alex Robbins is an illustrator and designer who graduated from Camberwell College of Arts, London. Now based in Berlin, he creates work for clients such as *TIME Magazine*, *The Guardian*, *Dazed and Confused*, Howies and *The New Yorker*.

Alexander Egger
satellitesmistakenforstars.com
A 22, A 27
Alexander Egger is a graphic designer, illustrator, concept developer, artist, writer, musician and publisher of artzines. He lives and works mostly in Vienna, Austria and in Gais, Italy. He works in different media on a range of cultural, commercial and self-initiated projects for either very small or very big clients. His work has been published in international magazines and books and he has had his work exposed in every continent except Antarctica. Monographs of his work have been published by Rupa Publishing and Rojo Editions.

Allistair Burt
holeinmypocket.com
A 26
Over the last few years, under the banner of Hole in my Pocket, Allistair has directed a series of short films for the UK's Channel 4, designed a 'Storytelling Machine', and exhibited artwork throughout the UK. His projects have also included creating a series of short books for the Glasgow International Art Festival and his self-initiated Small World Experiment. In 2009, Allistair was the creator of the design competition Common of Houses, which tried to solve the fiasco of British MPs' expenses through creative means.

Alvin Lustig
alvinlustig.com
See foreword p. 6
Alvin Lustig (1915–1955). Although it is more than half a century since his death, Alvin Lustig's influence can still be felt, and seen, in contemporary graphic design. Perhaps best known for his ground-breaking book jacket designs of the 1940s – with their use of expressive typography, simple line-art illustrations and photographic collages – Lustig also designed buildings, furniture, interiors, exhibitions, title sequences and, famously, a helicopter. A sense of honesty permeates Lustig's graphic design work. His stripped-down compositions and direct approach was in line with modernist ideals of the time and, along with Paul Rand, Lusting helped bring these principles to American graphic design. Alvin Lustig also played an important role in design education, teaching in the USA at Black Mountain College, the University of Georgia and Yale University.

Amandine Alessandra
amandinealessandra.com
A 13, A 14, A 15, A 16, A 17
Amandine Alessandra is a French photographer and graphic designer based in London. After a Masters in Fine Arts and Aesthetics from the Université de Provence in 2003, she moved to the UK, where she has run her own photographic practice since 2007. She graduated with a Masters in graphic design from the London College of Communication in 2009 and now works as a freelance graphic designer. Her three-dimensional typographic installations confront words and real life. Using context as a playground, the installation becomes a readable experience: contextual letterform is used as a medium for reinterpretation, reinforcing an obvious meaning or opening it up to a new perspective.

Andrew Byrom
andrewbyrom.com
A 38, A 39, A 40, A 41, A 42, A 43
See foreword pp. 6–9
Andrew Byrom was born in 1971 in Liverpool, UK. He graduated in 1996 from the University of East London. He worked briefly in the design department of Routledge, a leading academic book publisher, before opening his own design studio in London in 1997. Around this time he also began teaching graphic design at the University of Luton and Central Saint Martins. In 2006, Andrew moved to Los Angeles to take up an Associate Professor position at California State University. He now divides his time between teaching, designing for various clients and playing with his sons. He has recently been commissioned to design typefaces and type treatments for *The New York Times Magazine*, *Du Magazine*, McGraw-Hill and *Elle Decoration*.

Anna Garforth
crosshatchling.co.uk
A 23, A 24, A 25
Freelance illustrator and environmental artist Anna Garforth is based in London, where she studied at Central Saint Martins. Since graduating, her creative practice (Abe) has grown in ways she never expected. Projects include working with natural media, such as her much-talked-about moss typography – a collaboration with Eleanor Stevens. Anna has, paradoxically, become more appreciative of nature since moving to the city.

Antoine+Manuel
antoineetmanuel.com
A 12
Antoine Audiau and Manuel Warosz met in art school in Paris. They soon decided to work together under the name Antoine+Manuel. They combine hand-drawing and computer illustration with their own typography and photography. They each explore their favourite fields and creative methods, resulting in an output which, although diverse, has an obvious unity. Moving from dance to fashion via contemporary art and design, the duo has defined a singular graphic style. They work in the areas of fashion (Christian Lacroix), home and interiors (Habitat, Galeries Lafayette, Domestic, BD Ediciones), publishing, contemporary dance, theatre and art.

April Larivee
See foreword p. 9
April Larivee was born and raised on a small farm surrounded by mountains in Northern California. Her design work draws on this rural upbringing, and on her study of ecology and agriculture. She worked for several years at West Coast Choppers, and is now a consultant for several clients and non-profit organizations. Her experimental designs have appeared in art galleries and featured in design publications.

Arslan Shahid
behance.net/thearslan
A 31
Graphic designer Arslan Shahid was born in Pakistan, but lived in Dubai until 2004 when his family moved to Canada. It was there that Arslan started his studies at Toronto-based Ontario College of Art & Design (OCAD).

AT.AW.
at-aw.com
A 27
Eric Cheung was born in Canada and currently works as an architect in Toronto. His side projects, under the label AT.AW., can be described as 'guerrilla urbanism', as he optimistically subverts the often neglected, mediocre and complacent urban condition with a series of small urban projects.

Atelier van Wageningen
ateliervanwageningen.nl
A 32
Atelier van Wageningen (AVW) is a (typo)graphic design studio based in Amsterdam, The Netherlands. Since 1995 they have worked for a large number of international organizations including publishing houses, fashion labels and cultural institutions. AVW's award-winning work has also been published internationally.

Autobahn
autobahn.nl
A 33, A 34, A 35, A 36, A 37
Dutch studio Autobahn was launched in Utrecht, the Netherlands, by Jeroen Breen, Maarten Dullemeijer and Rob Stolte – all graduates from the Utrecht School of the Arts (HKU). Autobahn's graphic projects often have an illustrative and typographic focus. This passionate and ambitious team take an analytical approach to start with, followed by a strong sense of form at the end of the process.

Axel Peemoeller

axelpeemoeller.com

A 28, A 29, A 30

Axel Peemoeller studied visual communications in Düsseldorf, Hamburg and Melbourne. He works as a freelance designer, art director and senior designer for different clients and studios. Depending on the project, he travels to wherever he is needed and works for small boutique clients and large corporations. He follows his mantra: *'Design with thought is good design and will last.'*

B

BANK

bankassociates.de

B 49

Berlin-based BANK is run by French–German duo Sebastian Bissinger and Laure Boer, along with one intern and some associated designers. They plan, develop and realize a wide range of design projects for cultural, institutional and commercial clients, and are interested in unique approaches.

Bela Borsodi

belaborsodi.com

B 44

Bela Borsodi was born in 1966 in Vienna, Austria. He studied fine arts and graphic design at the Akademie für Angewandte Kunst before becoming a photographer. When he started to work for magazines he focused on shooting portraits and some reportage. Bela also experimented with 'light painting'. He moved to New York in 1992 and started to focus on still life photography in 1999, which remains the main direction of his work to date.

Benoit Lemoine

benoitlemoine.eu

B 47, B 48

French freelance graphic designer Benoit Lemoine studied in Belgium at the Institut St Luc, Tournai, and at the Graphic Research School in Brussels, from where he graduated in 2007. Since then Benoit has worked for numerous graphic design studios in Canada and Belgium including Studio Feed, Speculoos Studio, Double-Echo Studio and Salutpublic Studio. In 2006, Benoit also co-founded the Repeatafterme collective together with Jonathan Préteux and Guillaume Ninove, who regularly collaborate with Cécile Boche with whom Benoit created the White Desk project featured in this book.

Bola Cooper

bolacooper.com

B 46

Bola Cooper studied graphic design and illustration at the University of the Arts London, where she specialized in experimental illustration. Outside of university, she also worked with the lead fashion designer of Les Chiffoniers, Leena Similu, designing clothing labels for her start-up collection, as well as exhibiting work in the USA with *Five to Nine Magazine*.

Bradley–McQuade collaboration

B 46

Graphic designers Jamie McQuade and Thom Bradley graduated from Kingston University in the UK. They are passionate about typography, photography, illustration, printmaking, installation and sculptural work and everything in between. The duo exhibited a conceptual photography installation at the late Paul Arden's Arden & Anstruther photography gallery in Petworth, UK. They have also contributed to the design and production of independent London fashion and culture magazine *Playground*.

Brent Barson

brentbarson.com

B 45

Brent Barson graduated from the USA's Brigham Young University in 1997 with a BFA in graphic design, and he has been designing in all media ever since. He graduated from Art Center College of Design, Pasadena, with an MFA in media design in 2003, which led him to his current post as an assistant professor in BYU's graphic design department. He creates websites and interfaces, corporate identities, posters, and all other forms of design, but his first love is creating motion graphics. He has created the opening titles to a variety of independent films, as well as creating all motion graphics for the Typophile Film Festival since 2006.

C

Charlie Hocking

charliehocking.co.uk

C 65

Charlie Hocking is a London-based graphic designer and art director. He graduated in 2010 from London College of Communication. He has worked with studios in both the USA and the UK, interning with Steven Harrington and Justin Kreitmeyer at National Forest in Los Angeles and at Village Green Studio in London.

Charlotte Cornaton

charlottecornaton.com

C 65

Freelance graphic designer, videographer and ceramics artist Charlotte Cornaton graduated in art direction and graphic design from ESAG Penninghen in Paris in 2009. She has also attended ceramics courses at Central Saint Martins in London.

Cheil USA

cheilusa.com

C 50

Established in 1992, Cheil USA is the North America Regional Headquarters of Cheil Worldwide – the 16th-largest advertising agency in the world – which is headquartered in Seoul, South Korea. Based in Ridgefield Park, New Jersey, Cheil USA has North American locations in Dallas, Texas; Toronto, Canada; and Mexico. Through passion for ideas and idea engineering, Cheil Worldwide is a full-service communications agency specializing in creative, media, interactive, promotions and event marketing.

Chris Tozer

christozer.com

C 61

Fascinated by the possibilities of typography as image, Chris Tozer began experimenting with three-dimensional type during the final year of his graphic design degree at University College Falmouth, UK. His experimental project culminated in a book called *XYZ: Spatial Typography*, which investigates the possibilities of giving type a spatial context.

Chris Wilkinson

nineteeneighty.co.uk shu.ac.uk

C 64

Chris Wilkinson is a graphic designer based in Sheffield, UK, specializing in print design, art direction and illustration. He works on a regular basis with Sheffield Hallam University. Some of the key projects he has worked on include the rebrand of Sheffield Institute of Arts and the identity for the annual Creative Spark degree show. In around 2007, Chris developed a passion for creating type in 3D and considers himself lucky to have been able to use it in a few projects since then.

Chrysostomos Tsimourdagkas

C 66, C 67

Chrysostomos Tsimourdagkas (BArch, University of Thessaly, 2005, MArch, Architectural Association, 2007) is a registered architect in Greece. He has worked as a graphic, industrial and architectural designer for several firms including Zaha Hadid Architects. His work has been promoted through lectures and exhibitions in Athens, Helsinki, Berlin, Chicago, London and New York. At the time of writing, Chrysostomos was pursuing a PhD at the Department of Architecture of the Royal College of Art in London, investigating ways in which typography can be incorporated into the architectural field. This study is being funded by the Greek State Scholarships Foundation.

Clotilde Olyff

C 58, C 59, C 60

Brussels-based graphic designer and typographer Clotilde Olyff has been an elected member of the AGI (Alliance Graphique Internationale) since 2004. Since 1993 she has been a lecturer at Brussel's Le 75 – École Supérieure des Arts de l'image. She also works as a freelancer for agencies, industry and the public sector. To date, Clotilde has designed 42 stamps for Belgium and is the author and editor of 62 books and five typographic games. She has also published fonts via Font Bureau, USA and ?Rebbels in Canada. Her work has been exhibited internationally, and she has also lectured across the world.

Conor & David

conoranddavid.com

C 56

Conor Nolan and David Wall are designers who work on print, interactive and identity projects in Dublin, Ireland. Conor studied at the National College of Art and Design, Dublin and the Elisava Escola Superior de Disseny, Barcelona, while David studied at the National College of Art and Design, Dublin and Lahti University of Applied Sciences, Finland. Both graduated in 2002. Since the duo founded their studio in 2006, the focus of Conor & David's work has been to create thoughtful, rational, content-driven graphic design for print and screen, for a wide variety of clients.

Corriette Schoenaerts

corrietteschoenaerts.com

C 60, C 62, C 63

Corriette Schoenaerts is a Belgian photographer based in Amsterdam. She graduated from the Rietveld Academy and has been freelancing ever since. She works in the fields of autonomous, fashion and commercial photography, refusing to draw any finite distinctions between these fields. Corriette doesn't use a single, unambiguous style or choice of subject, choosing instead to research the message itself. According to her, a recognizable style is *'a cheap trick that fails to bring pleasure to yourself, your work or the public.'*

Craig Ward

wordsarepictures.co.uk

C 51, C 52, C 53, C 54, C 55, C 57

Craig Ward is a New York-based designer and typographer who likes playing with words. Having graduated in 2003 from Buckinghamshire Chiltern's University in the UK, he now operates under the moniker 'Words are Pictures', bringing life to headlines and constantly exploring the notion of type as image. He was named as one of the Art Directors Club of New York's Young Guns for 2008, and in 2009 received a certificate of Typographic Excellence from the Type Directors Club. For the most part he works alone, but he is collaborating more and more; he uses other people's skills to realize his increasingly complex ideas.

D

Daryl Tanghe

dtanghe.com

D 68, D 70

Daryl Tanghe grew up in Metro Detroit, Michigan. He attended the College for Creative Studies, where he learned how to design and relearned how to think about the world. Upon graduating from CCS, he moved from Detroit to Seattle, Washington, where he currently resides and works at Microsoft on the Windows team.

Dave Wood

thisisdavewood.co.uk

D 69

In 2005 Dave moved to London and began his graphic design education at Kingston University. The diversity of the course allowed him to explore and develop a portfolio that bridged new media, product design and film. After being nominated for the D&AD student awards in 2008, Dave gained experience in numerous studios including GBH and Johnson Banks, before going to work as a designer for The Partners. He is currently involved in a healthy mix of projects from small independent ones to international-scale jobs. He also pursues self-initiated projects in his spare time, and is currently indulging a passion for screenprinting and traditional processes.

David Aspinall

david-aspinall.com

D 70

David Aspinall is a London-based creative designer who enjoys experimenting with different media and materials. He graduated from Central Saint Martins in 2007. David relishes working with 3D materials, getting his hands dirty and finding solutions to the problems his ideas create.

Denise Gonzales Crisp

D 68

'Bi-located' in Los Angeles, California and Raleigh, North Carolina, Denise Gonzales Crisp is a professor of graphic design at North Carolina State University and designer of the occasional studio SuperStove!. Her designs and writings have appeared in many international publishing venues, including *Emigré*, *Items*, *Form*, *Design and Culture Journal*, *Design Observer* and *Eye Magazine*; in anthologies such as *All Access: The Making of Thirty Extraordinary Graphic Designers* and *Design Research: Methods and Perspectives*; and in exhibitions, including Dimension+Typography and East Coast/West Coast: Graphics in the United States. She holds an MFA from the California Institute of the Arts.

Detail. Design Studio

detail.ie

D 70

Detail. Design Studio is a creatively led design and communications company that was established in 2005. They specialize in identity, print communications and interactive design projects – large and small, simple and complex. Detail believe in analysis, simplicity, clear messages and original output. They help their clients develop a clear and consistent vision for their brand, products, services and environments.

Dolly Rogers

dollyrogers.com

D 71

Creative agency Dolly Rogers was founded in 2008 by Jennette Snape and Chris Costuna, both originally from Australia. The designers met while living in Amsterdam, where they are now based. Jennette and Chris believe that market research is not done behind a desk – they live the culture that they create for. They create visual communication concepts that are printed, that appear on screen, that make sound, that are silent, some that are bigger than you and others that can fit in your pocket.

E

Ed Nacional

ednacional.com

E 73

Ed Nacional is a graphic designer, type geek and recent graduate from Parsons the New School for Design. He is originally from Canada but now happily calls Brooklyn home. Ed designs for both print and the web, but also gets his hands dirty with printmaking techniques like silkscreen, gocco and letterpress.

Efsun Senturk

E 74

Originally from Istanbul, Turkey, Efsun Senturk is a freelance graphic designer based in Shoreditch, East London. She graduated from London College of Communication in 2007.

Elfen

www.elfen.co.uk

E 74

Guto Evans is a co-founder of Elfen, a design and branding company based in Cardiff Bay, Wales. Formed in 1997, the company has built a reputation for creating successful design and branding projects for a wide variety of clients. The company has a team of six multi-disciplined creatives working within the media, arts and cultural sectors.

Émilie Chen

emiliechen.ovh.org

E 72

Paris-based graphic designer Émilie Chen graduated in 2008 from the DSAA, ESAAB college in Nevers, France. After an internship at the design agency ODD in London, she went back to Paris to work in a small agency.

Emeline Brulé

E 77

Originally from France, Emeline Brulé moved to Brussels, Belgium, in 2009 to start her studies in visual communication, graphic design and typography at graphic research school ERG.

ÉricandMarie

ericandmarie.com

E 76

ÉricandMarie – Marie and Éric Gaspar – live and work in Paris. They teamed up in 2002, but have known each other and worked together since the early days of their graphic design education. After a first qualification in France, they obtained a Bachelor of Arts from Central Saint Martins College and a Masters degree from the Royal College of Art in London. They have carried out commissions for the Royal College of Art, the Dutch Ministry of Social Affairs and Employment, the Musée des Arts Décoratifs in Paris, the Villa Noailles in Hyères, Ronan and Erwan Bouroullec and the Mémorial de la Shoah in Paris.

Ersin Han Ersin

ersinhanersin.com

E 75

Freelance graphic designer Ersin Han Ersin is based in Ankara, Turkey. He has won several awards for his poster designs, which have been exhibited internationally.

Evelin Kasikov

evelinkasikov.com

E 78, E 79

Evelin Kasikov is an artist and designer. Born in Estonia, she now lives and works in London. Her work crosses the boundaries between handmade and digital. She creates typographic illustrations by fusing modernist design principles, technology and craft. By transforming printing processes into hand-embroidery, her work is influenced by craft but retains the context of graphic design. In 2008 she graduated from the MA communication design course at Central Saint Martins in London. She works as an independent designer, specializing in handmade type, typographic illustration and editorial work.

F

Fajn Hajp Agency
fajnhajp.com
F 85
Filip Bojovic is the founder of this Serbian design agency, which is based in Novi Sad, Vojvodina.

Farina Kuklinski
farinakuklinski.de
F 80, F 81
Berlin-based graphic desiger Farina Kuklinski studied at the Academie Beeldende Kunsten (Academy of Fine Arts) in Maastricht, the Netherlands, from where she graduated in 2009.

Ferdinand Alfonso
flux26.com
F 82
Ferdinand Alfonso is a graphic designer based in New York City. He graduated from the California College of Arts (and Crafts) in San Francisco/Oakland with a BFA in graphic design.

FL@33
F 88, F 89
See biography on page 240.

Fluid
fluidesign.co.uk
F 84, L 138
See also Lee Basford's biography. Birmingham-based Fluid was launched in 1995. Fluid is not only their name but also their branding philosophy. There is no house style, and the studio represents a rich pool of outstanding talent from a wide range of artistic disciplines. The company ethos 'Never Not Creating' ensures that every project they undertake benefits from an ingrained passion and cultural knowledge, earning Fluid a growing reputation for consistently evolving creativity.

Form
form.uk.com
F 83
Form is an award-winning London-based design company founded by Paul West and Paula Benson in 1991. They work in graphic design and branding for music, media, education and contemporary culture. They are driven by a passion for design and the power it has to make a difference to their clients and their products and services. Their innovative approach has resulted in effective and creative design solutions for identities, print and digital. Their work is frequently featured in design magazines, books and blogs, and the partners often lecture on design and culture.

Frost*Design
frostdesign.com.au
F 86, F 87
Frost is an internationally awarded creative studio founded by Vince Frost in 1994. Based in Sydney, Australia, the Frost team focuses on delivering real and enduring results for their clients. They work on anything from postage stamps to the built environment. The studio's collective skills and experience allow it to work seamlessly across a variety of media for a diverse range of international clients. Central to Frost's philosophy is the value and power of the 'Big Idea' and the difference it can make to a business, large or small, when correctly executed.

Funda Cevik
fundacevik.com
F 85
Turkish graphic designer Funda Cevik was born in Stuttgart, Germany. She graduated from Bilkent University in Ankara, Turkey in 2007 with a degree in graphic design before moving to Edinburgh to obtain her MFA degree in the same discipline at the Edinburgh College of Art.

G

Gareth Holt
garethholt.com
G 92
Independent designer and art director Gareth Holt runs his own studio in London, UK. He is a graduate of Camberwell College of Art and completed a Masters degree at the Royal College of Art. Conceptually driven, ideas-led design is fundamental to his approach and practice. He often collaborates with other designers on projects, and is a visiting lecturer at Chelsea College of Art and UCA Epsom.

Geoff Kaplan
generalworkinggroup.com
G 93
USA-based designer Geoff Kaplan of General Working Group has produced projects for a range of academic and cultural institutions, including MOCA, the Walker Art Center and CalArts. His work is in the permanent collection of the San Francisco Museum of Modern Art. He is senior adjunct professor in design at California College of the Arts.

Georgina Potier and Itamar Ferrer
georginapotier.com
ifita.com
G 90
Georgina Potier completed her BA in illustration at Kingston University, UK, and her MA in communication design at Central Saint Martins in London. She is an award-winning designer and conceptual thinker, whose strengths lie in bridging the gap between illustration and design, working in 2D and 3D to create quirky and thought-provoking images. The project *Earth Will Survive* shown in this book was a collaboration between Georgina and designer Itamar Ferrer. Itamar is from Venezuela and also obtained an MA from Central Saint Martins in 2007. Itamar now works with diverse clients including Research Centres Design Against Crime and Textile Futures from University of the Arts London.

Gluekit
www.gluekit.com
G 91
Gluekit is the illustration and design team of Kathleen Sleboda and Christopher Sleboda. Working from their home studio in Guilford, Connecticut, Gluekit creates illustrations, graphics and type treatments for clients around the world. In addition to their commercial work, the pair is passionate about their self-initiated projects. These range from typographic explorations to image and language play, experiments with visual narration and spatial relationships, and illustrations involving baby animals, pop stars, bricks and hearts. Gluekit's work has been exhibited in Japan, the UK, the Netherlands and the USA. In 2007 the pair established Part of It, a project that works with artists to create products for causes they are passionate about.

Go Welsh
gowelsh.com
G 90
Go Welsh is a design studio based in Lancaster, Pennsylvania, USA. They produce advertising, graphic design and public relations projects. Their widely published work has also been exhibited in New York at AIGA, the One Club, the Time Square Alliance, in Milwaukee at the Eisner American Museum of Advertising and Design, in the Morrison Gallery at Penn State Harrisburg, and is included in the permanent archives of the Denver Art Museum. Their work has also been part of travelling exhibitions in Canada and China.

H

HandMadeFont
handmadefont.com
H 100
Estonian design company HandMadeFont was founded in 2008 by Vladimir Loginov and Maksim Loginov. They specialize in developing unique, untraditional fonts. Their website offers hundreds of beautifully crafted fonts that can be purchased and used freely for any purpose from business cards to outdoor advertisements.

Handverk
madebyhandverk.no
H 106, H 107, H 108, H 109
Handverk is a small design company based in a small snowy town in the Norwegian countryside. The company was formed in 2009 by Eivind S. Platou (formerly Fruitcake Oslo) and Kåre Martens (formerly of Sopp Collective). As the name Handverk (Norwegian for 'hand craft') suggests, they approach most projects with a tactile and handmade sensibility.

Happycentro
happycentro.it
H 102, H 103
Graphic design studio Happycentro was launched in 1998 in Verona, Italy. The studio's approach to design is always the same: designing a logo, an advertising page, a wall or directing a commercial offers the same opportunity to deal with a problem. Mixing complexity, order and fatigue is their formula for beauty. In addition to their commissioned work, they always spend time and energy in research and testing.

Hat-trick
hat-trickdesign.co.uk
H 110, H 111
Multi-disciplinary studio Hat-trick Design was formed in 2001. They currently have ten staff based in their offices in London. They work for a wide variety of clients and, at the time this book was compiled, they ranked number two in *Design Week*'s creative survey. Their aim is to provide their clients with the highest standard of creative design and project management. They believe that the best way to achieve this is by the directors being very hands-on and leading the jobs from the front.

Helen Mycroft

helenmycroft.co.uk

H 104

Helen Mycroft is a creative from Sydney who splits her time between her two home countries of Australia and England. She studied at the University of Lincoln (School of Art and Design), UK, graduating in 2008 with a BA in graphic design. She won the YCN and Clearchannel student awards while there. Her work is a mix of pattern, type and love; it combines illustration and graphic design with strong ideas to create something that has concept and thought as well as being visually appealing.

Helena Dietrich

workwithhelena.com

H 104, H 105

Helena Dietrich is based in Stuttgart, Germany, where she works as a freelance graphic designer. She also works on self-initiated networking projects, such as Vow, a shop and gallery in Stuttgart, and a magazine that she co-edits and art-directs with Denise Amann.

Hijack Your Life

hijackyourlife.com

H 94, H 95, H 96

Hijack Your Life, aka Kalle Mattsson, lives and works in Amsterdam, the Netherlands, although he originally hails from Uppsala, Sweden. In the past he has worked freelance and in-house, focusing on illustration and graphic design.

Hoax

hoaxhoaxhoax.com

H 101

Hoax is a graphic design studio based in Utrecht, the Netherlands. It was founded by Bram Buijs, Steven van der Kaaij and Sven Gerhardt after their graduation from the Utrecht School of the Arts (HKU). All three are passionate about typography, materials and experimentation. Their main goal in graphic design is to steadily broaden their horizons, and they constantly try to renew their way of working by doing all sorts of experiments. They believe that every assignment deserves its own unique approach, resulting in its own individual visual translation.

Horst

horstphorst.com

See foreword p. 9

Horst P. Horst (1906–1999), most often known just as 'Horst', was a German-American photographer best known for the images of women and fashion he made for *Vogue* magazine. Horst began his association with *Vogue* in 1931, publishing his first photograph in the French edition of the magazine in November of that year. His first exhibition was shown in La Plume d'Or in Paris in 1932. A positive review appeared in *The New Yorker* after the show was over, and it made Horst instantly famous. Horst made a portrait of film star Bette Davis the same year, the first in a series of many celebrities that he would photograph during his life.

Hort

hort.org.uk

H 104

Berlin-based Hort (formerly known as Eike's Grafischer Hort, which was launched in 1994) is run by Eike König. Hort is a direct translation of the studio's mission – a creative playground and a place where 'work and play' can be said in the same sentence. Hort is an unconventional working environment. Once a household name in the music industry, it is now a multi-disciplinary creative hub. It is not just a studio space, but an institution devoted to making ideas come to life; a place to learn, a place to grow, and a place that is still growing.

HunterGatherer

huntergatherer.net

H 97, H 98, H 99

HunterGatherer is a New York City-based design, illustration, animation and production studio founded by Todd St. John. It has earned international recognition for its spare but inventive projects, which often combine experimental and hand-built techniques with more complex methods. Since 2000, HunterGatherer has stayed decidely small, focusing on a limited number of assignments across a wide range of media.

Huy Vu

weeboo.org

H 105

Graphic designer Huy Vu obtained an MFA in graphic design from the Rhode Island School of Design. He now lives in his home town of New York City and works for Jack Spade, designing everything from prints and patterns to special projects. Prior to all of this, he graduated from Carleton College with a BA in biology, upon which he sought employment as a janitor, a dance music publicist and a web producer at Listen Up!.

I

Intercity

intercitystudio.com

I 112

Intercity is a London-based graphic design studio with a network of collaborators from the worlds of art, design, illustration, photography and more.

Italo Lupi

italolupistudio.com

I 113

Born in 1934, Milano-based graphic designer Italo Lupi has an academic background in architecture, having studied at the Politecnico di Milano, Italy. He is a member of AGI (Alliance Graphique Internationale), an honorary member of the Art Directors Club of Milan, and was awarded the title of HonRDI (Honorary Royal Designer for Industry) in London. Exhibitions of Lupi's works have been held in New York, Tokyo, Osaka, Grenoble and Echirolles.

J

J. Kyle Daevel

kyledaevel.com

J 132

J. Kyle Daevel is a Chicago-based designer and artist. He received an MFA in 3D design from the Cranbrook Academy of Art in Bloomfield Hills, Michigan, and a BFA in graphic design from the University of Memphis in Memphis, Tennessee. His studio focuses on experimental 2D and 3D design, including furniture, products, graphic design and public art. Many of his 3D experiments draw upon his past professional 2D work. Typography, pattern and iconography are 2D topics that he consistently revisits within 3D archetypes.

Jack Curry

hitheremynameisjack.com

J 125

Freelance graphic designer and photographer Jack Curry is from Orange County, Florida, and studied at California State University, Long Beach. His Dash house number project, featured in this book, was awarded Judge's Top Honors for Student Work by the Type Directors Club 2009 Annual.

Jamie Hearn

jamiehearn.com

J 117

This London-based graphic designer graduated from Central Saint Martins College of Art and Design in 2010. Hearn won the 2004 Designer of the Future competition run by the Design Museum, London. He has worked for the creative agencies Landor, LagoStudio, Italy and Johnson Banks.

Jan Olof Nygren

joy-o.com

J 128

Jan Olof Nygren obtained a BFA from the School of Design and Crafts in Gothenburg, Sweden, where he also grew up. After successfully applying for a Fulbright grant he then studied for two years at the 2D design program at Cranbrook Academy of Art in Michigan and received an MFA degree. His previous work experience included a one-year position as a graphic designer at Ó! in Reykjavík, Iceland. He now works as a freelance graphic designer, illustrator and typographer and splits his time and work between Europe and the USA.

Jan von Holleben

janvonholleben.com

J 117

Jan von Holleben is an artist and photographer who lives and plays in Berlin. He is internationally known for his project *Dreams of Flying*. Jan grew up in an alternative commune in the south of Germany. He loves the mountains, muesli and herbal tea. For his education and the development of his work, he spent seven years in London, which he enjoyed and hated at the same time. He works across all fields of design for galleries, magazines and advertising. However, his passion lies within the photo-book-making world, where he can apply the ideas of the Homo Ludens, the man who learns through play, at its best with great publishers.

Jarrik Muller
jarrik.com
J 129, J 130
Jarrik Muller runs a design studio in Amsterdam, and occasionally works with international collaborators. He graduated in fine arts in graphic design in 2007 from the Willem de Kooning Academy in Rotterdam. Jarrik specializes in printed media, creative concepts, art direction, graphic design and typography.

Jenna Burwell
jennaburwell.blogspot.com
J 131
Graphic designer Jenna Burwell graduated from Lincoln University, UK, in 2010. Before this she studied general art and design at Oxford and Cherwell Valley College. Her work mainly consists of making and creating, photographing and then taking this into a graphic format.

Ji Lee
pleaseenjoy.com
J 133
Born in Seoul, Korea, and raised in São Paulo, Brazil, Ji Lee moved to New York to study graphic design at Parsons School of Design. After his studies, Ji worked in the fields of design, art, branding and advertising. Ji now works as the creative director at Google Creative Lab in New York, an in-house branding and marketing department at Google. Ji is the founder of the Bubble Project and the author of two books: *Talk Back: The Bubble Project* (Mark Batty, 2006) and *Univers Revolved: A 3-Dimensional Alphabet* (Harry N. Abrams, 2004). Ji's work has appeared in *ABC World News*, *The New York Times*, *Newsweek*, *Wired*, *Boing Boing* and *Gizmodo*, among others.

Jim Stevens
jstevensstudio.com
workroommolloy.com
R 187 (under Ryan Molloy)
Jim Stevens was raised in Raleigh, North Carolina. After a BA degree from Savannah College of Art and Design he got a Master of Architecture degree from North Carolina State University and the American Institute of Architects' Henry Adams Medal for Excellence in the Study of Architecture. Jim now has a full-time tenure track appointment at Lawrence Technological University, College of Architecture and Design in Southfield, Michigan. Along with his faculty appointment, he maintains a digital fabrication and design studio in Detroit, Michigan. Jim has published and lectured in the US, China and the Middle East.

João Henrique Wilbert
exquisiteclock.org
J 126, J 127
João Henrique Wilbert is a Brazilian multi-disciplinary media artist and researcher with interest and experience in interaction, design and programming. Over the last few years he has created and developed web and installation-based projects that engage with the use of technology as a medium for collaboration and creative expression. João has also worked as art director and web programmer for commercial brands worldwide. He is currently involved with research in the fields of tactical media, viral networks and reverse engineering.

Johanna Bonnevier
johannabonnevier.com
J 125
Johanna Bonnevier works as a freelance graphic designer based in London, although she is originally from Sweden. She is a former Central Saint Martins student. Since graduating, she has worked mostly with exhibition design/signage and books but also with printed matter. Her clients have included B-store, the Embassy of Sweden and Färgfabriken art space. Johanna frequently collaborates with 42/architects; under the name of weare42 they also work on joint projects that lie somewhere between graphic design and architecture.

John Morgan studio
morganstudio.co.uk
J 114, J 115
From the typography department at Reading University in the UK, John Morgan assisted Derek Birdsall at Omnific, London. In 2000 he established John Morgan studio, where he works with a small team on Platform 1 of Paddington Station. Alongside studio work, he has tutored at Central Saint Martins and the University of Reading, and co-founded Workplace Co-operative 115 with Robin Kinross, a new building for designers and makers. Morgan's projects include prayer books for the Church of England, granite poetry for the BBC, exhibition design for the Design Museum, art direction for Phillips de Pury, and a new graphic identity for David Chipperfield Architects. He has written for various journals, including *Typography Papers* and *Dot Dot Dot*.

Jonathan Hall
deadleaves.co.uk
J 118
Jonathan Hall studied graphic design at Glasgow School of Art, graduating in 2007. Originally from Northern Ireland, Jonathan now lives and works in Glasgow. Since graduating he has worked as a freelance designer/illustrator on both commissioned and self-initiated projects. His work deals largely with the physical and aesthetic qualities of old books and ephemera, using the familiar visual language of this material to create something distinctive and new.

Jörger-Stauss
joerger-stauss.ch
J 114, J 116
Theres Jörger studied visual communication at the Lucerne School of Art and Design, Switzerland. She graduated in 2001, having conducted research into typography and space. Theres now works freelance in Zürich. Since 2002 she has worked regularly in collaboration with the photographer Susanne Stauss. Susanne studied textile design and photography at the School of Art and Design Zürich, and since graduating has worked as a freelance photographer. Her focal point is artistic documentary photography. Work featured in this book includes both Theres's solo work and her collaborations with Susanne.

Juan Camilo Rojas
camilorojas.net
J 119, J 120, J 121, J 122, J 123, J 124
Colombian-born graphic designer Juan Camilo Rojas graduated from New World School of the Arts in Miami, USA, where he is now based. He considers his typographic work and experiments as an art form that enables him to communicate social awareness.

Juan Pablo Cambariere
cambariere.com
J 124
Juan Pablo Cambariere studied graphic design at Buenos Aires University, Argentina, where he is based. He is one of the most renowned South American book designers and his work has been featured in publications around the world. Juan is also a sculptor; he studied fine arts at the Buenos Aires Fine Arts Academy and worked for seven years as an assistant to Argentinian sculptor Enio Iommi. From a combination of both experiences, he developed *Essay on Power*, a 'family' of wooden puppets that he built to represent the whole of society.

Jung Eun Park
jung-park.com
J 131
Jung Eun Park is a freelance illustrator based in South Korea. She studied illustration at Central Saint Martins, London, from where she graduated in 2007.

K

Kari Szentesi
See foreword p. 9
Kari Szentesi was born and raised in San Diego, California. Her graphic design work is experimental in nature – playing with expectations, and asking the viewer to look closer.

Karin von Ompteda
quantitativetype.com
K 136, P 179
Karin von Ompteda is a doctoral researcher at the Royal College of Art, London, investigating typeface design for people with visual impairments. She continues to engage in self-initiated and commercial typographic design projects alongside her PhD work with clients including *Fortune Magazine* and Research RCA. Karin has lectured at international conferences including at ATypI 2008 and Include 2009. She has won awards for her research including the Commonwealth Scholarship (United Kingdom) and a Doctoral Fellowship from the Social Sciences and Humanities Research Council of Canada. Work featured in this book includes Karin's solo work and a collaboration with Peter Crnokrak.

Karina Petersen
karinapetersen.com
K 136, K 137
Graphic designer Karina Petersen from Denmark holds an MA in graphic design and is a 2009 graduate from Kolding School of Design, Denmark. In 2009 a book on her typographical work was published. Previously she has had work published in various design publications. Her work is characterized by an experimental and artistic approach, from minimalistic typographical compositions to abstract visual experiments, using collage, drawing, typography and photographs.

233

Kate Lyons
iamkatelyons.co.uk
K 134
London-based freelance graphic designer Kate Lyons graduated from Central Saint Martins in 2007. To date, her clients have included two publishers, a museum, a gallery, an artist, an exhibition designer, an events venue, a college, a library, a church, a pub and friends. Her work is mainly print-based and often typographic, and she regularly collaborates with her previous tutor Phil Baines. She especially enjoys designing books.

Kris Hofmann
krishofmann.co.uk
K 134, K 135
Originally from Austria, Kristina Hofmann moved to London in 2003. She holds a Masters degree from London's Royal College of Art, from where she graduated in 2009. She works as a freelance designer and director from her East London studio. She has a particular interest in experimenting with handmade techniques and their application to animation and typographic design. The building of sets and the use of tangible materials to play with the idea of what is 3D and 2D, real or not, is a recurring motif in both her print and moving-image work.

L

Lee Basford
www.meisai.co.uk
L 138, F 84
See also Fluid's biography.
Lee Basford is the art director at Fluid in Birmingham, UK, and works in and around the overlap of art and design, producing work for arts, video games, fashion and music companies. He has written and illustrated for the magazines *Paper-Sky, Dazed and Confused, Tokion* and *Level*; designed typefaces for T26 and Fountain, and exhibited internationally both as a solo artist and a member of the Outcrowd. His work has been featured in numerous books and design journals. In 2007 he was invited by Uniqlo to their Creative Awards in Japan, where he received a Judges Choice Award.

Lee Stokes
leestokes.co.uk
L 138
Originally from Stoke-on-Trent in the UK, Lee Stokes is now based in London, where he works freelance under his moniker StokeS.

Lisa Rienermann
lisarienermann.com
L 139
Originally from Cologne, Germany, freelance designer and photographer Lisa Rienermann now lives and works in Berlin. In 2005 she spent a semester in Barcelona. It was here that she created her project *Type The Sky*, for which she won awards and international recognition in 2007 and 2008. Lisa graduated from Folkwang Hochschule in 2008.

Louis Danziger
See foreword p. 6
New York City-born Louis Danziger (b. 1923) began his design education in high school and in Federal Art Project classes from 1938 to 1942. During 1946 through 1948, after military service in the Pacific, he continued his education, studying with Alvin Lustig and Alexey Brodovitch. He began his design practice in Los Angeles in 1949. His work includes art direction, advertising concepts and design. His work has been widely published and his clients have ranged from minuscule enterprises to major international corporations. A design educator for more than 50 years, he currently teaches at Art Center College of Design in Pasadena. He has taught at Chouinard Art Institute, been the director of the design program at California Institute of the Arts (CalArts) and taught at Harvard University, Carpenter Center (1978–88). He has given lectures and workshops at major universities throughout the USA as well as in Canada and Japan. Most notably, he pioneered the teaching of graphic design history in the USA. Elected to membership of the Alliance Graphique Internationale (AGI) in 1974, he has also received the Distinguished Achievement Award from the Contemporary Art Council of the Los Angeles County Art Museum in 1982, the Distinguished Designer Fellowship Award from the NEA in 1985, and was awarded the AIGA Medal in 1998.

M

MAGMA Brand Design
magmabranddesign.com
M 157
MAGMA Brand Design is an agency with a focus on corporate and brand design. It regards design as means to communicate information, values and attitudes; a way of evoking feelings and triggering thoughts and actions; and a method for breathing life into brands. Design is currently a general discipline that manifests itself in the interaction between society, companies and the market. MAGMA Brand Design supports corporate design processes and conducts projects in various branches and different media.

Marian Bantjes
bantjes.com
See foreword p. 7
Marian Bantjes has been variously described as a typographer, designer, artist and writer. Working from her base on a small island off the west coast of Canada, her personal, obsessive and sometimes strange graphic work has brought her international recognition. Following her interests in complexity and structure, Marian is known for her custom typography, detailed and lovingly precise vector art, her obsessive hand-work, and her patterning and ornament. Her work has been published in books and magazines around the world. She has lectured on her work throughout the USA and in many other countries, including South Africa, Argentina, Norway, France and New Zealand. In 2010, she spoke at the renowned TED Conference at Long Beach, California. In 2008, she was accepted as a member of the prestigious international design organization, Alliance Graphique Internationale (AGI). In the same year a monograph of her work was published as part of the bilingual *design&designer* book series by Pyramyd Editions, France. Her book *I Wonder* was published in 2010 by Thames & Hudson.

Mario Hugo
mariohugo.com
M 147
Mario Hugo is a New York-based artist and designer. Although he spends an inordinate amount of time in front of his computer, Mario still feels most honest with a pencil and two or more sheets of paper.

Marion Bataille
M 158, M 159
Paris-based Marion Bataille is a freelance graphic designer of book covers, typography and illustration. She graduated from ESAG Penninghen in Paris in 1980 and published her first book, *Livre de Lettres* (Editions Thierry Magnier), in 1999. Her popular alphabet pop-up book *ABC 3D* was released by numerous publishers around the globe in 2008.

Mark Formanek
formanek.de
standard-time.com
datenstrudel.de
M 142, M 143
German artist Mark Formanek lives and works in Münster and Berlin. The project *Standard Time* featured in this book was conceived by Mark and realized in collaboration with Jörn Hintzer and Jakob Hüfner of online broadcaster Datenstrudel. Datenstrudel (set up with a dozen like-minded artists in 2000) have streamed interactive web shows, realized music videos, directed TV commercials, and written and produced long and short feature film. They live and work in Berlin and released Mark's *Standard Time* as a DVD – a real-time 24-hour screensaver.

Me Studio
mestudio.info
M 148, M 149, M 150, M 151
Me Studio is a small graphic design studio that was founded in 2005 in Amsterdam by Martin Pyper, a British designer who has lived in the Netherlands since 1989. Martin studied at art school in the UK and speaks fluent Dutch.

Merci Bernard
mercibernard.fr
thinkexperimental.fr
M 153, M 154, M 155, M 156
French graphic designer Thomas Bernard graduated from the École Supérieure d'Arts Appliqués de Bourgogne (ESAAB). He founded Merci Bernard in 2007 and is also a member of the French graphic design collective Think Experimental.

Mervyn Kurlansky

kurlanskydesign.dk
M 141

Educated at Central School, London, 1960, Mervyn co-founded Pentagram in 1972 and set up Mervyn Kurlansky Design in 1994. His clients include multinational corporations, cultural establishments and educational institutions worldwide. He has won numerous design awards and was inducted into the South African Hall of Fame in 2006. His work is in the permanent collection of MoMA, New York, and has been featured in publications and exhibitions worldwide. He is the co-author of several books on Pentagram and design-related subjects. Active in design education, Mervyn lectures extensively and serves on design juries internationally. He is the past President of Icograda, Fellow of CSD, ISTD and RSA, and a member of AGI and Danish Designers.

Mesh Design

meshdesignltd.com
M 152

Mesh Design are a small but passionate collection of graduates based in the Midlands, UK. Formed in 2008, they combined their varying skills to create one company. Their collaborative approach and passionate enthusiasm for design has allowed them to work on a number of branding, advertising and website design projects for national companies. In their own words, *'The office is like a jostling hotbed of arguing enthusiasts. All this creative energy means that the projects we work on are delivered as seen through an educated, aesthetically invigorated eye.'*

Michael Hübner

micha-huebner.de
M 146

Michael Hübner was born in Leipzig, Germany. He began his design studies in the Bauhaus town of Dessau and explored various fields of creation. During this time he spent 14 months in France, where he studied art and communication for one semester in Angoulême and worked in Paris for Dream On. After graduating, Michael moved to Berlin to work for Minigram. In 2009 he moved to Basel, Switzerland, where he started a Masters in visual communication and iconic research at the Basel School of Design. In his research studies he explores how images work and focuses on spatial relations and representations like maps or panoramic pictures. Alongside his research, Michael continues to work as a designer.

Michelle Jones

wix.com/mich1980/mich web
M 146

Michelle Jones graduated from Central Saint Martins in 2004. She is passionate about 3D and hand-drawn type in her work.

Miguel Ramirez

www.holamr.com
M 140, M 144, M 145

Miguel Ramirez is a Los Angeles-based designer. Through his studies at California State University, Long Beach and in Basel, Switzerland, and his work experience at Art Center College of Design, he has developed an interest for experimental typography. Miguel continues to express his passion for type through various three-dimensional works.

Milton Glaser

miltonglaser.com
See foreword p. 7

Milton Glaser (b. 1929) is one of the most celebrated graphic designers in the USA. He has had one-man shows at MoMA, New York, and the Georges Pompidou Center, Paris. In 2004 he was selected for the lifetime achievement award of the Cooper Hewitt National Design Museum. As a Fulbright scholar, Glaser studied with the painter Giorgio Morandi in Bologna, Italy, and is an articulate spokesman for the ethical practice of design. He opened Milton Glaser, Inc. in 1974, and continues to produce an astounding amount of work in many fields of design to this day.

Miranda van Hooft

maddesign.nu
M 145

Miranda van Hooft is based in the Netherlands. In 2004, she graduated as an art director from the Willem de Kooning Academy, Rotterdam, and in 2009 as a graphic designer from the Royal Academy of Arts, the Hague.

MoreGood

moregood.co.uk
waterform.moregood.co.uk
M 160, M 161

MoreGood is home to the work of Ralph Hawkins and Amy Ricketts. MoreGood was set up in 2009 after the duo's graduation in graphic communication. MoreGood also teach part-time at the University for the Creative Arts, Farnham.

N

Nathan Gale

N 164
See Intercity for biography.

Nemanja Jehlicka

epicmewlynslab.blogspot.com
N 163

Nemanja Jehlicka was born in Belgrade (then still part of Yugoslavia) and was raised in Paris, France. He is the son of a graphic designer and a cultural attaché, and graduated from Paris's Lycée Technique Auguste Renoir in 2000. Nemanja is now based in Belgrade, where he works as a freelance art director, type designer and illustrator.

Non-Format

www.non-format.com
N 162

Kjell Ekhorn (Norwegian) and Jon Forss (British) have worked together as the creative direction and design team Non-Format since 2000. They work on a range of projects including art direction, design, illustration and custom typography for arts and culture, music industry, fashion and advertising clients. They have art-directed the independent music monthly *The Wire* and also *Varoom*, the journal of illustration and made images. Their first monograph was published in 2006 by Pyramyd Editions as part of the bilingual *design&designer* series. In 2007 a hardback monograph entitled *Non-Format Love Song* was published by Die Gestalten Verlag, a second edition was released in 2008. Non-Format are based in Oslo, Norway and in Minneapolis, USA.

NR2154

nr2154.com
N 165

Established by Jacob Wildschiødtz and Troels Faber, NR2154 is a multi-disciplinary design studio based in Copenhagen and New York. Troels and Jacob have worked together since 1996 when, at the age of 20, they launched a skateboard magazine. This was followed by a music and lifestyle magazine in 1998. That same year they completed their first client design projects, and they set up the design studio, which in 2005 changed its name to NR2154. The name NR2154 is a project number, underlining the ethos that the project always comes first. This focus is also evident from the studio's variety of solutions, including both overall visual identities and the implementation of individual elements such as exhibition designs and books.

O

Oded Ezer

odedezer.com
O 166, O 167, O 168, O 169

Oded Ezer is an award-winning graphic designer, type designer, design educator, pioneer in the field of 3D Hebrew lettering and a typographic experimentalist who invented the term 'biotypography'. Oded's projects, posters and graphic works are showcased and published worldwide, and are part of the permanent collections of eminent museums such as MoMA, New York, Israel Museum of Art, Jerusalem, and the Museum für Gestaltung Zürich, Switzerland. Oded studied at the Bezalel Academy of Art and Design, Jerusalem from 1994 to 1998. In 2000 he set up his own independent studio, Oded Ezer Typography, in Givatayim, where he specializes in brand identity, typographic design and Hebrew and Latin typeface design. He also teaches typography and graphic design at H.I.T. (Holon Institute of Technology), and at the Wizo Haifa College of Design, and gives lectures in academies and conferences outside Israel. Oded's first monograph, *Oded Ezer: The Typographer's Guide to the Galaxy*, was published by Die Gestalten Verlag in 2009.

Open Studio

weareopenstudio.de
O 169

Julia Furtmann and Kai Hoffmann live and work together in Düsseldorf, Germany. After graduating from the Institute of Design, and gaining valuable work experience in several agencies and studios, they decided to set up their own studio in 2009. The Open Studio is a multi-disciplinary studio for visual communication that combines a design studio, a gallery and an advertising agency. It found its home in a small storefront with a tiny shop window, which is the perfect place to work, show self-initiated work and collaborate with other designers and artists.

P

Paul Elliman
wikipedia.org/wiki/Paul_Elliman
See foreword p. 9
Paul Elliman is a London-based artist and designer. He designed the typeface Found Font, derived from an ongoing collection of industrial parts in which no letterform is repeated. Elliman also engages the human voice in many of its social, technological and linguistic guises, from popular songs to public announcements and radio broadcasts. *Sirens Taken for Wonders*, a project commissioned for the New York biennial Performa09, initiated a series of discussions about the coded language of the city's emergency vehicle sirens. Paul has exhibited widely in venues such as Tate Modern in London, Kunsthalle Basel in Switzerland, New York's New Museum for Contemporary Art, and APAP in Anyang, Korea.

Pesca Salada
polviladoms.com
P 172
During the daytime, Barcelona-based Pol Viladoms Claverol works as an architect, while Maria Beltran Marín organizes events and conferences. In their spare time, however, they work as graphic designers and photographers under the moniker Pesca Salada.

Peter Crnokrak and Karin von Ompteda
theluxuryofprotest.com
P 179, K 136
Peter Crnokrak is a London-based designer and creative director of The Luxury of Protest. A primary focus of Peter's work is data visualization, with a particular interest in the intersection of visual semiotics and data analysis. His work has been exhibited at InfoVis, bio.21, Computational Aesthetics and SIGGRAPH. The Luxury of Protest has been featured in more than 60 books and magazines, and has won a number of international design competitions, including the European Design Awards and AIGA 365. Work featured in this book includes one of Peter's collaborations with Karin von Ompteda, alongside Karin's solo work.

Piero Glina
pieroglina.de
P 175
Originally from Germany, Piero Glina is a Zürich-based communication designer. His specific interest is in the areas where different media and different ways of communication overlap. He gained recognition with several award-winning projects in the fields of video and printed matter, and his works have been exhibited internationally. Piero is co-founder of Telekolleg, an independent space for art and music. He also founded The Magic Shadow Boys in 2000, a group of visualists who try to bridge the gap between music and film in a live music environment. The Magic Shadow Boys have performed alongside the likes of Kraftwerk-member Karl Bartos, Âme, Carl Craig, Mark Stewart and Angie Reed.

Plasticbionic
plasticbionic.com
P 178
Julien Brisson has been working as a graphic designer since 2004. Based in Nantes, France, he is driven by his passion for art and typography. In 2006, he joined Fly Designers as an art director/graphic designer, where he became involved in interactive design. He has since carried out commissions for music labels, clubs, public institutions and business societies. He also works freelance under the moniker Plasticbionic.

Pleaseletmedesign
pleaseletmedesign.com
P 176, P 177
Pleaseletmedesign (PLMD) is a graphic design studio set up in Brussels, Belgium, in 2004 by Pierre Smeets and Damien Aresta. They started the studio directly after quitting school (they studied typography at ERG, Brussels), and decided to learn everything else in the field instead. In 2009, their regular collaboration with Morgan Fortems led to the creation of a second studio in Nancy, France. PLMD's projects include graphic design, exhibition design, signage, title sequences and websites.

Post Typography
posttypography.com
P 173, P 174, P 175
Post Typography is a Baltimore-based studio specializing in graphic design, conceptual typography and custom lettering/illustration, with additional forays into art, apparel, music, curating, design theory and vandalism. Post Typography's work has received numerous design awards, been featured in books, and their posters are collected by high-school punk rockers and prominent designers (whom they consider equally important). In between working for clients such as the *New York Times* and the U.S. Green Building Council, Post Typography have authored and designed *Lettering & Type: Creating Letters and Designing Typefaces* (Princeton Architectural Press, 2009). A bilingual monograph of the studio's work was published by Pyramyd Editions as part of their *design&designer* book series.

Praline and RSHP Model Shop
designbypraline.com
P 170, P 171
Praline was created in 2000 by David Tanguy, fresh out of London's Central Saint Martins. Today it is a five-strong (and growing) design studio based in London. Praline works for international clients on various projects from art direction, corporate identities, web and exhibition design through to print and book design. They have won several international awards, including the Chicago 100 Show for web design, the D&AD award for environmental design, the Fedrigoni Award for educational brochures and the Art Directors Club of New York award for corporate literature.

R

R2
r2design.pt
R 182
Lizá Ramalho and Artur Rebelo formed the design studio R2 in 1995. Based in Porto, Portugal, R2 works on projects for cultural organizations, contemporary artists and architects in areas such as visual identity, poster, book, signage, graphic installation and exhibition design. Lizá and Artur have lectured in graphic design since 1999, have co-ordinated various workshops and participated as speakers and jury members in numerous national and international events. They have been invited to a wide array of international exhibitions and their projects have been published in specialized books and design magazines. R2 have won several international awards and Lizá and Artur are both Alliance Graphique Internationale (AGI) members.

Rafael Farias
rafaelfarias.co.uk
bumfcollective.com
R 183, R 184
Rafael Farias is a graphic designer and artist from London. He gained a BA from the University for the Creative Arts in Maidstone, Kent, and now works as a freelance graphic designer. Past achievements include being shortlisted for the Penguin Design Awards and receiving a D&AD in-book award. Rafael is also a member of Bumf, an art collective that he set up with friends from university. Bumf is an ongoing, online exhibition of creative output, which involves the creation of work following rules set by others in the collective.

Raphaël Legrand
experimentationsgraphiques.
blogspot.com
ilssemarierent.com
R 190, R 191
Raphaël Legrand graduated from ESAAB in Nevers, France, in 2002 before moving to Paris, where he now works as a freelance graphic designer. He avoids working with his computer whenever he can and enjoys all aspects of photography. He is member of the design collective Ils Se Marièrent.

Rebootlab

rebootlab.com

R 182

German designers Tim Faulwetter and Peter Werner share an interest in the dynamics of urban subcultures. It is this curiosity that has been the catalyst for their collaboration since they first met in 1998. After working together on different projects, they joined forces in 2001 and set up rebootlab.com. Since then, they have worked together on intercultural and intermediate design projects. The majority of their work focuses on developing design for interactive media, illustration and graphic design. Like the subcultures, rebootlab.com is constantly reinventing itself; it is both hideout and design laboratory at the same time.

Rick Myers

art-utility.com

R 187

Myers Art-Utility is a design company formed in 2010, building on commissioned artwork made since 1996. Books designed by A-U have been exhibited internationally, and are included in numerous special collections such as MoMA, New York, Tate Gallery, London and Kunsthaus Zürich.

Rinzen

rinzen.com

R 188, R 189

The Australian art and design group Rinzen is perhaps best known for the collaborative approach of its five members, forming as a result of their *RMX* project in 2000. Rinzen's work, created both individually and as a collective, covers a wide range of styles and techniques, often featuring utopian alternate realities, bold, geometric designs or intricate, hand-drawn studies. 'Play' is a key role in their creative process, creating work that is cheerful, optimistic and celebratory. Rinzen is Steve Alexander and Rilla Alexander in Berlin; Adrian Clifford in Brisbane; Craig Redman in New York; and Karl Maier in Melbourne.

Roger Excoffon

wikipedia.org/wiki/Roger_Excoffon

See foreword p. 7

Roger Excoffon (1910–1983) was a French typeface designer and graphic designer. Excoffon was born in Marseilles, studied law at the University of Aix-en-Provence, and then moved to Paris for an apprenticeship in a print shop. In 1947 he formed his own advertising agency and concurrently became design director of a small foundry in Marseille called Fonderie Olive. Later he co-founded the prestigious Studio U+O (a reference to Urbi et Orbi). Excoffon's best-known typefaces are Mistral and Antique Olive; the latter he designed in 1962–1966. Air France was one of Excoffon's largest and most prestigious clients. The airline continues to use a customized variant of Antique Olive in its graphic identity. Excoffon's faces have an organic vibrancy not found in similar sans-serif types of the period. His typefaces gave voice to an exuberant body of contemporary French and European graphic design.

Rowland Scherman

rowlandscherman.com

R 180, R 181

Rowland Scherman was born in New York in 1937. He studied art at Oberlin College when he realized he wanted to be a photographer. He served as the first photographer for the Peace Corps in 1961, helping to give the newly formed agency its image. Rowland went freelance in 1964. His work has been published on the covers and in the pages of *Life*, *Time*, *Paris Match*, *Newsweek*, *Playboy* and *National Geographic*. While living in the UK, he photographed the alphabet in human form – Love Letters – the project featured in this book. In 1968, he won a Grammy award for the cover of *Bob Dylan's Greatest Hits*, and published a photo book called *Elvis is Everywhere* in 1991. He currently lives in Cape Cod, Massachusetts. He photographs the landscape and accepts portraiture assignments.

Ryan Molloy

workroommolloy.com

R 185, R 186

Ryan Molloy is a freelance designer, artist, and an assistant professor of graphic design at Eastern Michigan University in Ypsilanti, Michigan. Prior to teaching at Eastern, he was a visiting lecturer at the University of Texas at Austin's design division, where he also received his MFA in design. He is an educator and inter-disciplinary designer, having practised in the fields of architecture and graphic design. His graphic design work has received numerous awards, including an ADC Young Guns Award. His work has been exhibited internationally including at the OneDotZero film festival in 2008.

S

s3studio

s3projects.com

S 212

Graphic designer Maxime Archambault graduated from CEGEP du Vieux Montreal, Canada, and now runs Montreal-based s3studio (aka S.3). Prior to setting up S.3 in 2005, he worked full-time developing designs for the fashion industry, including work for Sims, Converse and Groggy.

Sagmeister Inc.

sagmeister.com

S 196, S 197, S 198, S 199, S 200

Stefan Sagmeister, a native of Austria, received his MFA in graphic design from the University of Applied Arts in Vienna and, as a Fulbright Scholar, a Masters from the Pratt Institute in New York. He formed the New York-based Sagmeister Inc. in 1993 and has since designed identities and graphics for Viacom, Warner Brothers, Bertelsmann as well as non-profit organizations such as TrueMajority and OneVoice. His work has been nominated five times for the Grammies and has won most international design awards. A book titled *Things I Have Learned in My Life So Far* was published by Abrams in 2008. Stefan lectures worldwide on design and branding.

Sakis Kyratzis

actual-size.net

S 210

Sakis Kyratzis was born and raised in Greece. He is a designer, photographer and interaction designer, working mainly with architects and the culture sector. After graduating from Central Saint Martins, London, he has worked for an architectural practice, but also undertakes freelance work. As a result, his work is quite varied: it includes projections for opera and dance performances, working with charities and community projects, designing books for photographers and websites for artists, doing promotional materials for exhibitions and the Central Saint Martins degree shows, and pursuing his own interests in photography and screenprinting. He is also an associate lecturer at Central Saint Martins. Prior to his career in graphic design, he obtained an MA and a PhD in linguistics.

Satsuki Atsumi

S 203

Satsuki Atsumi was born in Shizuoka, Japan, in 1978. She grew up in traditional Japanese culture, which included Chinese calligraphy. Satsuki combines her cultural background and fine art experience in her simple and conceptual designs. She moved to California in 2004, where she graduated from California State University, Long Beach.

Sean Freeman

thereis.co.uk

C 54, C 55, S 210

Sean Freeman was born in Gibraltar and used to sell suits for Paul Smith. Since finishing his degree in 2007, Sean Freeman has been producing semi-photographic type treatments and illustrations for a wide range of clients. His work derives from his love for playing and his endless enthusiasm for experimenting with out-of-the-ordinary materials, including acrylic paint mixed with hair gel, powder, milk, ink in water, and smoke. Sean Freeman's clients include *The New York Times Magazine*, VH1, *Wired*, HarperCollins, *Computer Arts* and *Digital Arts*.

Sean Martindale

smartindale.com

S 192, S 193, S 194

Sean Martindale is an inter-disciplinary artist and designer currently residing in Toronto, Canada. His interventions, which frequently focus on ecological and social issues, activate public and semi-public spaces to encourage engagement. His playful work questions and suggests alternate possibilities for existing sites, infrastructures and materials found in urban environments. Often intentionally ephemeral and encountered by accident, his interventions engage others in city spaces.

Sebastian Gagin

ablank.com.ar

S 202

Born and raised in Buenos Aires, Argentina, graphic designer Sebastian Gagin graduated from the University of Buenos Aires in 2009. He takes pictures, plays in a band, draws, and tries to get himself involved in as many independent design projects as possible.

Sebastian Lemm

sebastianlemm.com

S 195

Sebastian Lemm, a native of Germany, relocated to New York City in 2000 after graduating from Berlin University of the Arts (MFA equivalent). Sebastian works as an independant graphic designer and visual artist in Brooklyn.

Sharon Pazner

flickr.com/photos/sharonpazner

S 202

Sharon Pazner was born in Kenya and spent her childhood in Jerusalem and in Washington, D.C. Sharon studied architecture in Jerusalem in the Bezalel Academy of Art and Design and at the Ecole d'Architecture, Paris, from where she graduated in 2001. Since then she has resided in Israel. Her work has been exhibited internationally.

Shotopop

shotopop.com

S 201

Shotopop was launched by Carin Standford and Casper Franken – both graduates of the University of Pretoria, South Africa. After relocating to the UK, they started freelancing and did Shotopop work in any spare time. Eventually they found that their own work was taking up all their time. They are now represented by Valerie Oualid and Wizz in France, from whom they get a large proportion of their work.

Simone Stecher

simonestecher.wordpress.com

S 211

Simone Stecher grew up in South Tyrol, Italy. She studied graphic design at the University of Wales, Newport.

Siobhan Tarr

hantwerc.de

S 202

Freelance mosaic artist Siobhan Tarr was born and grew up in England. She then lived in Australia before moving to Germany, where she has lived since 1993 in the countryside between Hamburg and Luebeck. Siobhan's work has been exhibited internationally.

Start

wearestart.com

S 204, S 205

Start is a collective, the vision of Phil Robson and Mat Carlot. Originally from London and Paris, they met in Sydney, Australia.

Stefan G. Bucher, 344 Design

344design.com

dailymonster.com

S 206

Stefan G. Bucher is the man behind 344 Design, and the online drawing and storytelling experiment dailymonster.com. His monsters have invaded computer screens all over the world, and their savage adolescence is chronicled in the book *100 Days of Monsters* (How, 2008). Stefan has created designs for Sting, David Hockney, Tarsem, and the *New York Times*, and works with a whole roster of brilliant, driven clients. His time-lapse drawings appear on the rebooted TV classic *The Electric Company* on PBS. He is the author of *All Access — The Making of Thirty Extraordinary Graphic Designers* (Rockport, 2004) and *The Graphic Eye — Photographs by Graphic Designers From Around The Globe* (Chronicle/RotoVision, 2009).

Strange Attractors Design

strangeattractors.com

S 208, S 209

Strange Attractors Design is the international studio of Ryan Pescatore Frisk and Catelijne van Middelkoop. Based in Rotterdam, the Netherlands, and in New York City, they create innovative ideas and solutions to influence culture and commerce. The duo are also active design researchers and educators, giving lectures and workshops around the globe. In the Netherlands they teach at the Design Academy, Eindhoven, and The Royal Academy of Art, the Hague. They also teach at Parsons New School for Design in New York.

Studio for Virtual Typography

virtualtypography.com

S 214, S 215

Matthias Hillner was born in Germany, where he trained first in photography, then in visual design. He received his MA in communication art and design from the Royal College of Art in London in 2001, and his MPhil in the same subject in 2007. Having worked for various design agencies in London, Matthias founded his Studio for Virtual Typography in 2005. This business development was supported by the National Endowment for Science, Technology and the Arts (NESTA) and the National Film and Television School in Britain. Matthias also works as a senior lecturer in graphic design at the University of Hertfordshire in England.

Studio Lundsager

studiolundsager.com

kongtukan.com

S 213

Studio Lundsager was set up by designer and art director Mikkel Lundsager Hansen. After finishing his BA in Denmark, he moved to London to complete his Masters in communication design at Central Saint Martins. After working as a freelancer on a range of projects, he joined the team at the prestigious design company Stylorouge, specializing in design for music. Mikkel now lives and works in London.

Studio Output

studio-output.com

S 206

Studio Output was set up in 2002 by three partners: Rob Coke, Dan Moore and Ian Hambleton. It is now a team of 13 run across two studios in London and Nottingham. Studio Output work on everything from branding and campaigns to websites and motion graphics. Their clients include Arts Council England, Sony PlayStation, the BBC, Ministry of Sound, Nokia and HMV.

Studio Xavier Encinas

xavierencinas.com

swisslegacy.com

S 204

Xavier Encinas is a French art director living and working in Paris, France. His work is focused on typography, editorial design and print collaterals. He is the design director of French fashion magazine *Under The Influence* and Canadian culture magazine *The Lab*. He is also the founder of the blog Swiss Legacy.

Stylorouge

stylorouge.co.uk

S 207

Stylorouge is an independent creative consultancy with more than 25 years' experience in commercial media. They work in the areas of graphic design and art direction, advertising, film and television, photography and multimedia. Stylorouge was founded by Rob O'Connor, who is the creative driving force of the studio. Rob is a graduate of Brighton Art College who started work as a designer/art director at Polydor Records. Within three years he had made the break and started Stylorouge from an uncompromising desire to create unique, effective design. It is Rob's enthusiasm for diversity that has led the business to expand its repertoire of services to all forms of new media, and in doing so has earned him a reputation as an art director and as a film and video director. He has been a visiting lecturer and external assessor at various art colleges.

Supermundane

supermundane.com

S 208

Supermundane is the pseudonym of Rob Lowe, who was born in the Midlands, England. Having worked in graphic design for more than 12 years, he has become known as an illustrator, art director, typographer and graphic artist. His graphic art, which depicts a utopian world of organic shapes and beasts displaying hope, melancholy and beauty, has been published and exhibited worldwide including several solo exhibitions. He is the creative director of the quarterly alternative children's magazine *Anorak*, and art director of the food quarterly *Fire & Knives*. He lives and works in London.

Superscript²

super-script.com

ink-magazine.com

S 204

Founded in 2006 in Lyon, France, by Pierre Delmas Bouly and Patrick Lallemand, Superscript² is a graphic design studio that outputs a variety of graphic design media including publishing (books, monographs, catalogues, magazines and posters), typography and digital media (websites and interactive installations). Since 2006, the studio has developed and produced a typographic magazine called *Ink*.

Sveta Sebyakina

sebyakina.ru

S 200

Sveta Sebyakina is a graphic designer, type designer and art director at the Republica design studio in Moscow. The studio works on a variety of projects including identity, branding and graphic design.

T

Thijs Verbeek

www.thijsverbeek.nl

T 216, T 217

Thijs Verbeek was born in Amsterdam, the Netherlands. After turbulent years at school he decided to go to the Art Academy in 2000. He studied graphic design at the HKU in Utrecht and graduated in 2005. He then held internships at studio Anthon Beeke, Swip Stolk, Lex Reitsma and Paulina Matusiak. He works hard to combine commissioned projects with free experiments.

U

Underware's Type Workshop

underware.nl

typeworkshop.com

U 218, U 219, U 220, U 221

Underware was founded in 1999 by Akiem Helmling, Bas Jacobs and Sami Kortemäki. They are based in Den Haag, Helsinki and Amsterdam. Together with Donald Beekman and Liza Enebeis, they set up the radio channel Typeradio in 2004. Underware also holds workshops at various academies and conferences worldwide. These workshops can be followed in real time online. The often spectacular output of these workshops has been published widely.

V

Vaughan Oliver

vaughanoliver.co.uk

V 222, V 223, V 224, V 225

Independent record label 4AD's identity was designed in 1980, and has been maintained by Vaughan Oliver and his collaborators for more than 25 years. Initially a collaboration with photographer Nigel Grierson, they were then called 23 Envelope. Nigel left in 1988. Supported by Chris Bigg since 1988, Oliver and Bigg's collaborative work is credited to studio v23 – the founding of which was the result of their creative partnership being formalized in 1998. Specializing in work for the music industry, their collaboration has attracted commissions for company identities, magazine design, books and book cover design, special print projects, print advertising, and promotional campaigns and film direction. A highly successful retrospective of Vaughan Oliver's work in Nantes, France, in 1992 resulted in shows in Paris, Tokyo, Los Angeles, the UK and Athens. Vaughan's work has been collected for London's Victoria and Albert Museum archives, and is on permanent exhibition in the museum's Twentieth Century Gallery. *Vaughan Oliver: Visceral Pleasures*, a design monograph by Rick Poynor, was published in 2000, and *Vaughan Oliver and v23 Poster Designs* was published in 2005. Vaughan is based in Epsom, England. He teaches at the University for the Creative Arts in Epsom and also gives lectures in the UK and abroad.

W

Wilfrid Wood

wilfridwood.com

W 226, W 227

Wilfrid Wood was born in London and grew up in Sussex, UK. He graduated from Central Saint Martins. After college he worked for a publishing company, then for the TV programme *Spitting Image*, a satirical show featuring puppets of public figures, as a head builder. He now concentrates almost entirely on 3D work; heads, figures and some lettering. His studio is in Hackney Wick. When he is not working on commissions, he creates self-initiated pieces that are shown on his website or at exhibitions.

X

Xavier Encinas

S 204

See Studio Xavier Encinas for biography.

FL@33

flat33.co

postcard-book.info
madeandsold.com
' type.com

FL@33 is a multi-disciplinary studio
for visual communication based
in London. Its two founders,
Agathe Jacquillat (French, fro___
Paris) and Tomi Vollauschek
but from Frankfurt, Germany)
studied at FH Darmstadt (Ge____
ESAG Penninghen (Paris), HI
(Gothenburg) and Camberwe____
of Art (London), before they ___
the Royal College of Art's po
graduate communication art
design course in 1999.

They set up their company in London
in 2001. The studio's clients include
MTV Networks, the BBC, the Royal
Festival Hall, Laurence King
Publishing, *Creative Review*, *Computer
Arts*, Groupe Galeries Lafayette,
Matelsom, Habitat, Penrhyn Books,
Weeks & Cowling, MMM-Festival and
Friends of the Earth.

magazines,
around the world. Interv___
duo appeared on BBC Radio and
NPR (America's National Public
Radio) after *The New York Times*,
along with its international
supplements, featured an article
about the bzzzpeek.com project.

FL@33 often judge competitions and
award schemes, including YCN, FITC,
D&AD and Selected in Barcelona. In
2010 they gave a talk at the Selected
A: Graphic Design from Europe
conference, which was organized by
Index Book.

___h was published
___he bilingual
___) *design&designer*
___amyd Editions.

___s conceived, compiled,
___ and designed by
___ been published by
___ing: *Postcard* appeared in
___owed by *Made & Sold: Toys,
___Prints, Zines and Other Stuff*
___9. *Postcard* was also translated
___ench (*Cartes Postales*, Pyramyd
___ons), German (*Postcard:
___stkarten-Design heute*, DuMont
___uchverlag) and Spanish (*Postales:
Diseño por correo*, Gustavo Gili).

Agathe and Tomi have designed
several other books, including
Laurence King's *200% Cotton: New
T-Shirt Graphics*, *300% Cotton: More
T-Shirt Graphics*; *Patterns: New
Surface Design*; and *Cult Streetwear*.

Acknowledgements

We would like to thank all of the
people who responded to the call
for entries for this book. We are
very grateful for the number and
quality of submissions we
received, which exceeded the
number of pages available to us.

Special thanks must go to our
publisher Laurence King and his
team, especially Helen Rochester,
Melissa Danny, Felicity Awdry and
Angus Hyland.

Another very special thanks must
go to Andrew Byrom for his help
and support in connection with
his insightful foreword.

We would also like to thank all of
the contributors who made their
valuable time available to us, to
point us in the direction of other
people's work, created or revised
artworks especially for the book
or prepared photoshoots for us.

Sincere thanks also to these
particularly inspiring and helpful
people: Alexander Egger, Arslan
Shahid, Atelier van Wageningen,
Andrew Byrom, Craig Ward,
Clotilde Olyff, Denise Gonzales
Crisp, Dolly Rogers,
HandMadeFont, Hoax, Italo Lupi,
João Henrique Wilbert, Joe
Shouldice at Sagmeister Inc.,
Jörn Hintzer at Datenstrudel,
Mervyn Kurlansky, Marion
Bataille, Nathan Gale, Oded Ezer,
Praline, Pleaseletmedesign,
Plasticbionic, Rowland Scherman,
Rafael Farias, Sean Martindale
and Vaughan Oliver.

And last but not least, we
would like to thank our
clients, collaborators and
supporters, especially our
families and friends.

If you would like to submit
your own tangible 3D type
for potential inclusion in
future editions of this book,
please visit our dedicated
website at 3d-type.com.